Popular Fish
in the
Mediterranean Sea

Stanley Farrugia Randon - Robert Micallef

Stanley Farrugia Randon
92, Kananea Str, Attard BZN 04
Tel: 9947 7806

Custom Lab Ltd
Olaf Gollcher Str,
Ta' Paris, B'Kara BKR 13
Tel: 21448746

First published 2004

ISBN: 99932-0-280-0

Printed by P.E.G. Ltd, San Ġwann, Malta

Introduction

The fishing industry has been in existence for a very long time, probably even more than agriculture. The importance of the fishing industry has however declined. Other industries grew in importance and young people started looking for more stable jobs on land. Throughout the ages fishing methods have changed, mainly because of more competition and an improvement in technology.

Although the importance of this industry has decreased, the advantage of including fish in our daily diet is recognized more than ever. Our country imports a lot of canned and frozen fish. The large amount of tourists visiting our islands demands a stronger fishing industry.

This handbook gives information on the most popular fish encountered by professional and amateur fishermen in the Mediterranean.

Stanley Farrugia Randon
Robert Micallef
September 2003

M: *Alonga*
E: *Albacore, Long Fin Tunny*
L: *Thunnus alalunga*

Size and weight: This fish reaches a length of 1.5m and a weight of 20kg.
Characteristics: The back of this fish is dark blue and its sides are silver. Its fins are yellowish.
Habitat: The Albacore lives close to the surface or mid-waters. It eats on smaller fish.
Alimentary value: Its meat is good, but that of the Tuna is considered to be better.
Fishing methods: During the past years it was noticed that the incidence of this fish in Maltese waters is increasing, especially around Filfla. It is caught mostly in gill nets which are called 'alalongara'. Amateur fishermen catch this fish by trolling with an artificial fish of between 10 and 20cm in length.

M: Aringa
E: Herring
L: Clupea harengus

Size and weight: This fish reaches a length of 60cm and a weight of about 1.5kg.
Characteristics: It has a large head and big eyes. Its scales are large.
Habitat: It is found in deep waters and it is a migratory fish. It enters shallow waters to lay eggs. This species is not very commonly found in Maltese waters, but it is heavily imported and is commonly used as bait by our fishermen.
Alimentary value: This fish is often cooked in batter and we find it imported as frozen fish.
Fishing methods: The Herring is caught in nets, but it can also be caught by trolling (*sajd bir-rixa*).

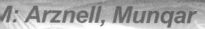

M: Arznell, Munqar
E: **Small-spotted Picarel**
..: *Spicara flexuosa*

Size and weight: It reaches a size of about 18cm and a weight of about 50g.
Characteristics: It is silvery-grey in colour and it has a black spot on each side. The fish has blue and green marks on its sides.
Habitat: The Picarel lives in mid-waters or near the sea bed.
Alimentary value: It is used to make fish stock and its meat is good.
Fishing methods: The Picarel trap is used. This is much larger then the Bogue trap. There is no need of any bait as it is believed that the fish enters to spawn in it. This fishing method is not popular any more, but in Gozo it is still much in use. Sometimes the Picarel enters the Bogue traps (*nassi tal-Vopi*). It is also caught by use of the fishing rod.

M: *Arznella tat-Tikek, Pajżana*
E: *Blotched Picarel*
L: *Spicara maena*

Size and weight: This fish reaches a size of about 22cm and a weight of about 100g.
Characteristics: It has an oval shape and it distinguished by a dark spot in the middle of its sides. It also has other small grey spots. The back of the fish is dark blue and its sides have a lighter blue colour.
Habitat: It is found mostly next to sandy sea beds.
Alimentary value: It is used to make fish stock and its meat is good.
Fishing methods: The Picarel trap is used (*Nassa ta' l-Arznell*). This is much larger then the Bogue trap. There is no need of any bait as it is believed that the fish enters to spawn in it. This fishing method is not popular any more, but in Gozo it is still much in use. Sometimes the Picarel is caught in the Bogue traps (*nassi tal-Vopi*) and fishing rods.

M: *Awrata*
E: *Gilthead Sea Bream*
L: *Sparus aurata*

Size and weight: This fish reaches a size of about 60cm and a weight of about 5kg.
Characteristics: The Sea Bream has a large head with a neatly arching forehead. It has a steely-grey skin with a characteristic golden band between the eyes. There are some yellowish streaks on its flanks.
Habitat: This fish lives near rocky sea beds.
Alimentary value: This is of great importance as this fish is exploited by the aquaculture industry.
Fishing methods: Together with the European Seabass this fish is the most common fish to be exploited by the aquaculture industry. It has become a popular fish in Malta when it started to escape from their nets. It is easily caught with a fishing rod. It enters very shallow waters and prefers shrimps as bait. Hooks size 10 and lines size 0.25mm are preferably used.

M: *Bakkaljaw*
E: *Poor Cod*
L: *Trisopterus minutus*

Size and weight: The Poor Cod reaches a length of about 20cm and a weight of about 200g.
Characteristics: The Poor Cod has an elongated body with a short barbel protruding from the lower jaw.
Habitat: It lives near coastal waters although it can also be found in deep waters.
Alimentary value: The Poor Cod is preferably cooked deep-fried in batter.
Fishing methods: The fishermen do not usually fish for the Poor Cod but it is often accidentally caught while fishing for other species.

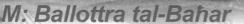

M: Ballottra tal-Bahar
E: Shore Rockling
L: Ophidion rocchei

Size and weight: This fish reaches a length of about 30cm and a weight of about 50g.
Characteristics: This is an elongated fish with a small head. It has a dark brown colour. Other species include the Cuskeel and the Ophedion.
Habitat: The Rockling lives on the sea bed, where it often hides in a hole.
Alimentary value: This is very low.
Fishing methods: The fishermen do not usually fish for the Rockling.

M:Barbun
E: Wide-eyed Flounder
L: Bothus podas

Size and weight: It reaches a length of about 50cm and a weight of about a kilogram.

Characteristics: Its body is flat and rounded. Its eyes are both on the left side of its body and are far wider apart than other species of this family. The fins originate from nearly all around the body. The head is marbled yellow. The left part of the body is brown with large pale spots ringed in yellow, blue or white. The right eyeless side is off-white.

Habitat: The Flounder often hides below sandy or muddy bottoms. It can be found in depths of between 10 and 200 metres or more.

Alimentary value: The meat of this fish is tender and delicious.

Fishing methods: Since this fish is found on the sea bed, the easiest way to catch the Flounder is by using the harpoon. Many times it is difficult to spot the fish because it covers itself with sand. It is also caught in trawl nets.

M: *Barbun Imperjali*
E: *Turbot*
L: *Psetta maxima*

Size and weight: It can reach a length of 1m and a weight of about 8kg.
Characteristics: This fish is flattened and has a broad body. Its eyes are on the left of its body and are close to each other. The colour varies from brown to grey but always matches the surroundings. It has a lot of dark spots and blotches.
Habitat: The Turbot often hides below sandy or muddy bottoms.
Alimentary value: The meat of this fish is tender and delicious.
Fishing methods: Since this fish is found on the sea bed, the easiest way to catch the Turbot is by using the harpoon. Many times it is difficult to spot the fish because it covers itself with sand. It is also caught in trawl nets.

M: *Bażuga*
E: *Axillary Sea Bream*
L: *Pagellus acarne*

Size and weight: It can reach a length of about 30cm and a weight of not more than 1kg.
Characteristics: Its body is slender and not so deep. It has a pink colour with a darker back and paler belly. There is a dark spot at the base of the pectoral fins.
Habitat: It is found near sandy sea beds.
Alimentary value: It can be used for fish stock, but it is not very popular.
Fishing methods: Although the fishermen do not fish for the Axillary Sea Bream, it is often caught by the use of a bottom line (*mitlaq*) hauled from a boat, inside pots (*nassi*) or caught in a net.

M: *Boll Komuni*
E: *Common Stingray*
L: *Dasyatis pastinaca*

Size and weight: This fish grows up to 2m in length and a weight of about 30kg.

Characteristics: The Stingray is a flat fish. Its tail is longer than that of the Ray. Just behind the origin of the tail stalk they possess a long barbed spine with venom-secreting glands on the lower side. Its colour is greenish-brown.

Habitat: The Stingrays are bottom dwellers, especially on sandy bottoms.

Alimentary value: It is an edible fish, but many people do not like its taste.

Fishing methods: The easiest way of catching the fish is by the use of the harpoon. The fish offers resistance and can also use its barbed spine to defend itself. It is mostly caught by bottom long-lines (*konz tal-qiegh*).

M: Budakkra Rasha Sewda
E: Black-headed Blenny
L: Tripterygion tripteronotus

Size and weight: This fish reaches a length of 8cm and a weight of about 10g.
Characteristics: The Blenny is a small and elongated fish, but its fins make it look bigger. It has a black head and wide bands placed vertically. It has a red body and is yellowish ventrally. Other species include the Peacock Blenny, the Red-speckel Blenny, the Tompot Blenny, the Horned Blenny and the Silver Clinid.
Habitat: It lives in shallow coastal waters.
Alimentary value: This is of little importance.
Fishing methods: Fishermen do not fish for the Blenny.

M: *Budakkra ta' l-Għajn*
E: **Butterfly Blenny**
L: *Blennius ocellaris*

Size and weight: This fish reaches a length of 20cm and a weight of about 40g.
Characteristics: This Blenny has a large head with prominent eyes and lips. The anterior section of the dorsal fin is made of ten to twelve spiny rays and is elevated at the front with three elongated rays. The dorsal fins possess a dark blue spot.
Habitat: This Blenny lives close to the sea bed.
Alimentary value: This is very low.
Fishing methods: This Blenny may be caught by amateur fishermen using a fishing rod.

M: Burqax
E: Painted Comber, Lettered Perch
L: Serranus scriba

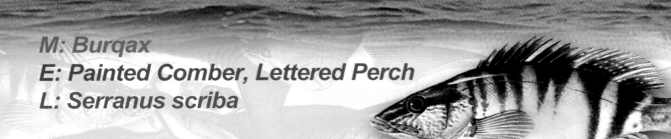

Size and weight: The Comber reaches a length of about 30cm and a weight of about 200g.
Characteristics: It has a yellowish-brown colour with vertical dark brown stripes. The cheeks have red and blue markings, resembling colourful scribblings.
Habitat: It lives close to the seabed in shallow or deep waters. It lives mostly in the shelter of sea grasses.
Alimentary value: This fish is often used for fish stock into which pieces of the fish may be placed.
Fishing methods: Since this fish lives close to the sea bed, the bottom long-line (*konz tal-qiegħ*) is the best way how to catch the fish. It has a large mouth and it easily swallows hooks size 4. Amateur fishermen use a long-line which is hauled from the boat.

M: Bużaqq
E: *Killifish*
L: *Aphanius fasciatus*

Size and weight: This small fish reaches a length of about 7cm and a weight of about 10g.
Characteristics: The Killifish has a small mouth which is deflected upwards. The male is smaller and yellow or greyish-green, with blue areas and about twelve dark vertical bands across the sides. The female is larger and more greyish, with alternating narrow and shorter black stripes.
Habitat: The Killifish is found in shallow water and eats on smaller fish or minute crustaceans.
Alimentary value: This is very low.
Fishing methods: This fish is caught using the rod with very small hooks.

M: Ċawla
E: Blue Damselfish
L: Chromis chromis

Size and weight: This fish reaches a length of 10cm and a weight of about 25g.

Characteristics: This is a small fish. It has a black to very dark brown colour. When young it has a bluish colour.

Habitat: It lives in shallow coastal waters.

Alimentary value: The Damselfish was used to make fish stock but its popularity is decreasing. Fish vendors used to offer the fish for sale in the streets.

Fishing methods: Many amateur fishermen start fishing with the aim of catching this fish; then they tend to become more ambitious! The Damselfish may be caught with the treble hook (*kulpara*). The fish are attracted to an area by spreading bread crumbs and then the treble hook is lowered into the sea. It is then retrieved quickly with the hope that one of the hooks pierces the belly of a fish. The Damselfish often enters the Bogue pot (*nassa tal-Vopi*).

M: Ċerna
E: Dusky Grouper
L: Epinephalus guaza

Size and weight: This fish grows about 1.5m in length and reaches a weight of about 40kg.
Characteristics: The Grouper has a large head and prominent eyes. It has a dark reddish-brown coloration, fading to a pale yellowish-brown underneath.
Habitat: This fish lives in caves and close to rocky sea beds.
Alimentary value: The Grouper has a delicious tender flesh.
Fishing methods: The Grouper can be caught in trawl nets (*xbieki tat-tkarkir)* and trammel nets (*pariti*). It is popular with spear-fishermen and many human fatalities, occurring during this type of fishing, were caused because this fish has the tendency of seeking refuge in deep caves. The fish is also caught by bottom long-lines (*konz tal-qiegħ*) especially close to the border of a reef. This fish has a large mouth and so hooks size 1 should be used, baited with whole fish. Unfortunately the Grouper is decreasing in number due to overfishing. A fisherman catching a small specimen of this fish should let it live.

M: Ċervjola
E: *Greater Amberjack*
L: *Seriola dumerili*

Size and weight: This fish can grow up to a metre in length and reach a size of about 25kg.
Characteristics: The Amberjack has a thick streamlined body, laterally compressed. It has a dark blue back. Its flanks are light silvery-grey and its abdomen is nearly white. Mature specimens obtain a yellowish coloration.
Habitat: The Amberjack is often seen swimming close to the surface chasing the Transparent Goby and the Common Sand Smelt which start to jump out of the water and sometimes onto the rocks. The mature specimens enter coastal waters in summer and autumn.
Alimentary value: The fish has a good-tasting flesh and is often served in restaurants.
Fishing methods: The Amberjack is caught in nets which are hauled close to the shore. It is also caught in the nets used to haul in the Dolphin Fish that gather around the *kannizzati* floats. Amateur fishermen prefer using a lure (*sajd bir-rixa*). A living fish or an artificial lure may be used. Others prefer using stripes of cuttlefish. These are hooked from one end and from the middle, while the other end is left free in order to imitate the wriggling movements of a fish's tail. The fish may also be caught by the use of the fishing rod.

M: *Ċinturin*
E: *Silver Scabbardfish*
L: *Lepidopus caudatus*

Size and weight: This is an elongated fish and can reach a length of 1.5m and a weight of 5kg.
Characteristics: This is an elongated fish, compressed at the sides. Its tail is small. It is grey in colour.
Habitat: It is a free-swimming inhabitant of the open sea.
Alimentary value: This fish is not as commonly marketed as it is in other countries such as Italy.
Fishing methods: It is caught with long-lines (*konzijiet*).

M: *Ċippullazza*
E: *Red Scorpionfish*
L: *Scorpaena scrofa*

Size and weight: Although it is very similar to the Black Scorpionfish, this fish is larger in size. It can reach a length of up to half a metre and a weight of about 2kg.

Characteristics: It has a rough back, full of spines, especially on its head. It has a rough skin. It is red in colour with brownish spots scattered around its body.

Habitat: It lives in depths of between 10-200m. It can be found on rocky, grassy or sandy bottoms.

Alimentary value: The Red Scorpionfish has a tender white flesh. It makes a delicious fish stock.

Fishing methods: Since it lives close to the sea bed, it is mostly caught in trawl nets (*xbieki tat-tkarkir*), or trammel nets (*pariti*) which are left to drift along the sea bed.

M: Ċippullazza ta' l-Għajn
E: **Rockfish**
L: *Helicolenus dactylopterus*

Size and weight: This fish reaches a length of less than half a metre and a weight of about 2kg.

Characteristics: It has a white body and a big head full of spines, and prominent eyes. It is red in colour with about six dark vertical bands on the sides.

Habitat: It can live in shallow waters, or in depths of up to 200m. It can be found on rocky, grassy or sandy bottoms.

Alimentary Value: The Rockfish has a tender white flesh. It makes a delicious fish stock.

Fishing methods: Since it lives close to the sea bed, it is mostly caught in trawl nets (*xbieki tat-tkarkir*), or trammel nets (*pariti*) which are left to drift along the sea bed.

M: Denċi
E: Dentex
L: Dentex dentex

Size and weight: This fish can reach a length of 1m and a weight of more than 10kg.
Characteristics: The Dentex has a large head and prominent eyes. Its colour is blue-grey and its fins are yellowish. The flanks have small red and blue spots. It eats on smaller fish.
Habitat: It is found over rocky sea beds, in caves or ship wrecks. It can live in shallow or deep waters up to 100m.
Alimentary Value: Its flesh is of fine quality and is popular with both Maltese and tourists.
Fishing methods: The best way how to fish for the Dentex is by the use of the bottom long-line (*konz tal-qiegħ*). The long-line is left for a few hours and between each hook a distance of about 10m must be left. The hooks should be between size 4 and 1, and pieces of Mackerel, Bogue, squid, octopus or cuttlefish may be used as bait. Underwater fishing is a challenging way how to catch this fish. Trolling (*sajd bir-rixa*) close to the sea bed may also prove to be an effective method.

M: Dott tal-Faxxi
E: Grouper
L: Epinephalus aeneus

Size and weight: This fish reaches a length of about 1m and a weight of about 30kg.
Characteristics: The Grouper has a large head and big jaws. It is grey in colour with a few light stripes behind the eyes and five or six faint dark vertical bands on the flanks. Other species include the Golden Grouper and the Dog-face Grouper.
Habitat: The Grouper lives close to rocky sea beds and inside caves.
Alimentary value: This fish has a delicious and tender flesh. It is often served at the best restaurants.
Fishing methods: This fish is the dream of every underwater fisherman. It is also caught in trammel nets (*pariti*), trawl nets (*xbieki tat-tkarkir*), bottom long-lines (*konzijiet tal-qiegħ*), and occasionally inside a pot (*nassa*).

23

M: Fanfru
E: Pilotfish
L: Naucrates ductor

Size and weight: The Pilot Fish can reach a length of about 40cm and a weight of up to 2kg.
Characteristics: The back is dark blue while the abdomen is whitish. The flanks are silvery with five or six broad vertical bands.
Habitat: The Pilot Fish lives close to the surface of deep waters. It is similar to the Dolphin Fish in that it prefers to shelter below floating objects.
Alimentary value: It has a tasty flesh although it is rather dry.
Fishing methods: The Pilot Fish is often caught together with the Dorado using the *kannizzati* fishing method. It is also caught by trolling (*sajd bir-rixa*), especially if a small artificial lure is used.

M: *Gallina Ghadma*
E: *Piper Gurnard*
L: *Trigla lyra*

Size and weight: This fish reaches a length of about 60cm and a weight of about 1kg.
Characteristics: The back of the Gurnard is red and the flanks are pinkish. It has a longitudinal body and a steep forehead.
Habitat: It is found close to the sea bed especially on sand.
Alimentary value: Its flesh is very good.
Fishing methods: It is usually caught by the use of long-lines or in trawl nets, and it makes a grunting sound when caught.

M: Gremxula tal-Baħar Ħalqha Għoli
E: Deep-nosed Pipefish
L: Syngnathus typhle

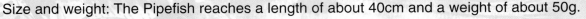

Size and weight: The Pipefish reaches a length of about 40cm and a weight of about 50g.
Characteristics: Its body is typically long and tubular, covered in stiff large scales. It has a brownish-green colour. This Pipefish has a long and laterally compressed snout that makes it different from other species such as the Short-snout Pipefish.
Habitat: It is found in both deep and shallow waters.
Alimentary value: This is not an edible fish.
Fishing methods: The Pipefish is not usually caught by fishermen.

M: *Gringu*
E: *Conger Eel*
L: *Conger conger*

Size and weight: The Conger Eel can reach a length of about 2m and a weight of more than 60kg.

Characteristics: This has a normal eel-shaped body, cylindrical, and circular in section. Its jaws are lined with close-packed, small but powerful teeth.

Habitat: It occurs most commonly in crevices and small caves, on rocky bottoms and inside wrecks. Its diet consists of small fish, crustaceans and crabs.

Alimentary value: The Conger Eel is edible but its serpent-like shape seems to prevent some housewives from including it in the menu.

Fishing methods: It is mostly caught with bottom long-lines (*konzijiet tal-qiegħ*), but it can be also captured using traps made of metal mesh (*barrada*).

M: *Gurbell tad-Daqna*
E: **Bearded Croaker**
L: *Umbrina cirrosa*

Size and weight: The Croaker reaches a size of about 50cm and a weight of up to 3kg.
Characteristics: The Bearded Croaker has a dark back with silvery grey or brown reflections. It is also decorated by diagonal wavy yellow lines alternating with blue reaching down and forwards to the flanks. It has an almost semi-circular back.
Habitat: This fish lives near the coast on rocky bottoms.
Alimentary value: The Croaker has a delicious flesh. It is however not often sold.
Fishing methods: It is caught in fishing nets and long-lines, however large species are caught by spear fishing.

M: *Gurbell Rar*
E: *Meagre*
L: *Argyrosomus regius*

Size and weight: The Meagre reaches a length of 80cm and a weight of about 6kg.
Characteristics: This fish has a greyish back and bronze flanks. Its abdomen is white.
Habitat: This fish lives near the coast on rocky bottoms.
Alimentary value: The Meagre has a delicious flesh. It is however not often sold.
Fishing methods: It is caught in fishing nets and long-lines, however large species are caught by spear fishing.

M: Gurbell Tork
E: Brown Meagre
L: Sciena umbra

Size and weight: The Brown Meagre reaches a length of about 40cm and a weight of about 3kg.
Characteristics: The Brown Meagre has a high, slightly deep body with an almost semi-circular back. It has a dark brownish-bronze colour.
Habitat: This fish lives near the coast on rocky bottoms.
Alimentary value: This Meagre has a delicious flesh. It is however not often sold.
Fishing methods: It is caught in fishing nets and long-lines, however large species are caught by spear fishing.

M: *Gharusa*
E: **Rainbow Wrasse**
L: *Coris julis*

Size and weight: The Wrasse reaches a length of about 25cm and a weight of about 150g.
Characteristics: The Wrasse has an elongated body and is a colourful fish. The female has red and brown colours. The male has more variable colours than the female, such as red, orange, yellow and brown, as well as blue and greenish spots. It has a very slippery skin.
Habitat: The Wrasse lives in deep and shallow waters on grassy bottoms. It is mostly caught on grassy reefs.
Alimentary value: It is used to make fish stock.
Fishing methods: The best method to catch this fish is by the long-line (*mitlaq*). Small hook sizes must be used as it has a small mouth. The fish is also caught in nets or by the use of fishing rods.

M: *Ħaddiela Komuni*
E: *Marbled Electric Ray*
L: *Torpedo marmorata*

Size and weight: The Ray can reach a length of 1m and a weight of about 1.5kg.
Characteristics: The body is a smoothly rounded disk with a short tail. Its eyes are small and close to each other. It may be coloured various shades of brown having a sandy appearance. It is armed with glands that can emit an electric shock.
Habitat: The Ray lives on sandy bottoms under which it can hide.
Alimentary value: This fish has a good flesh.
Fishing methods: Amateur fishermen can catch the Ray by harpoon fishing. It is also caught in trawl nets (*xbieki tat-tkarkir*).

M: Ħanżir tal-Fond
E: Wreck Fish
L: Polyprion americanum

Size and weight: The Wreckfish reaches a length of about 2m and a weight of about 50kg.
Characteristics: This fish has a large head with wide jaws. It has a grey back. Its sides are brownish-grey with irregular pale patches.
Habitat: The Wreckfish lives close to rocky sea beds and in caves.
Alimentary value: This fish has a fine flesh and is often sold as Grouper.
Fishing methods: Underwater fishing will be very rewarding if a fisherman catches a large specimen of the Wreckfish. It is also caught by trammel nets (*pariti*), trawl nets (*xbieki tat-tkarkir*), and bottom long-lines (*konzijiet tal-qiegħ*).

M: *Hmar*
E: *Triggerfish*
L: *Balistes carolinensis*

Size and weight: The fish reaches a length of about 50cm and a weight of about 5kg.
Characteristics: The Triggerfish has an oval shape and is covered in large rough scales. Its eyes and mouth are relatively small. It has a grayish-brown colour. Underwater fishermen claim that the Triggerfish is fearless and allows them to touch it.
Habitat: The Triggerfish lives in depths of between 1m and 40m.
Alimentary value: The flesh of the Triggerfish is not usually edible but some amateur fishermen sustain that it all depends on how it is cooked.
Fishing methods: It is caught by a line hauled from a boat (*mitlaq*) and by underwater spear fishing.

M: *Ħuta Kaħla*
E: *Blue Shark*
L: *Prionace glauca*

Size and weight: This shark can reach a length of 5m and a weight of about 600kg.
Characteristics: This fish has a brilliant indigo-blue back fading to pure white at the belly.
Habitat: It lives in mid-waters far out at sea, but can also swim close to the coast.
Alimentary value: This is of little importance.
Fishing methods: This fish is often caught in trawl nets (*xbieki tat-tkarkir*) and gill nets (*għeżula*). It may also be caught with the surface long-lines (*konzijiet tal-wiċċ*) used to catch the Swordfish and Tuna. Some amateur fishermen venture to catch this fish by using a particular technique. The fisherman holds a rod that is connected to a large buoy from which a metal cable projects vertically towards the sea bed. To this metal cable are tied large hooks that are baited with whole fish.

M: Imsella
E: Garfish
L: Belone belone

Size and weight: The Garfish can reach a length of about 1m, but will not weigh more than 700g. This is because it has a slim body.

Characteristics: The Garfish has a long and slim body. It has an elongated head tapering into a fine pointed snout bearing numerous fine teeth. It has a silver-grey colour with a black back and a whitish abdomen.

Habitat: In summer it lives close to the surface while in winter it seeks deeper waters.

Alimentary value: Although the Garfish is considered to be of scarce market value, larger specimens can be grilled.

Fishing methods: A fishing rod of about 5m in length and a fishing line of 0.18mm in diameter are required. The hook must be small, for example size 12. No float or weight should be used. The best bait is pieces of raw Bogue. The amateur fisherman should bite a piece of the latter fish, chew it and then hook it to the line. The hook should then be lured (*trejjex*) on the surface of the sea until the Garfish snatches it. When the Garfish opens its pointed jaws to snatch the bait and starts offering resistance, the rod must be jabbed and the fish hauled out of the water straight away. At this point the fish starts to twist and turn energetically to the amusement of onlookers. Trolling from a boat can also catch the Garfish. They love bacon. Since the fish swims close to the surface, it can also be caught by a long-line which has a small sail and is let out to sea with the wind from a rocky beach (*mrejkba*).

M: Inċova
E: Anchovy
L: *Engraulis encrasicolus*

Size and weight: It grows up to a length of about 20cm and a weight of about 150g.
Characteristics: This fish has a slender body. It has an olive-green back and silvery flanks.
Habitat: It lives in shallow waters and it is very common in Malta.
Alimentary value: The fish is tasty and is usually preserved in brine.
Fishing methods: The Anchovy is caught by using large nets (*tartarun*). This is the same method used to catch the Sardines.

M: Kahlija
E: Saddled Bream,
   Black-tailed Bream
L: Oblada melanura

Size and weight: The fish reaches a length of about 30cm and a weight of about 800g.
Characteristics: As a member of the Sparide family, it has a moderately deep and flat body. It has small jaws and prominent eyes. The Bream has silvery flanks with a blue iridescence. Before the tail there is a black spot and this makes it easily recognizable to the inexperienced fisherman. The fish reproduces in spring.
Habitat: The Saddled Bream is found mostly close to rocky coasts, facing the sea currents. It is best caught when the sea is slightly rough.
Alimentary value: This fish has a very good flesh. In Malta it is considered to be a delicious fish.
Fishing methods: It is most commonly caught from the coast by use of the fishing rod. It may however also be caught by the use of a small float which are attached hooks (*forka*), by trolling from a boat (*sajd bir-rixa*), or by the use of a long-line which is carried seawards by means of a sail (*mrejkba*). Professional fishermen make use of nets such as the trammel (*parit*), and gill nets (*xketti*).

M: *Kastardella*
E: *Atlantic Saury, Saury Pike*
L: *Scomberesox saurus*

Size and weight: The Pike reaches a length of about 50cm and a weight of about 1kg.
Characteristics: This is an elongated fish, similar to the Garfish, but it is more cylindrical. It also has thin and pointed beak-like jaws.
Habitat: It is occasionally common and found close to the surface.
Alimentary value: The Saury Pike has a good taste, but is not commonly found in the housewife's menu.
Fishing methods: The most effective way how to catch the pike is by the use of large gill nets (*għeżula*). It can also be caught by trolling (*trejjex*).

M: Kavall
E: Atlantic Mackerel
L: Scomber scombrus

Size and weight: This fish reaches a length of more than 50cm and a weight of about 2kg.
Characteristics: The Mackerel has an elongated spindle shape, a pointed head and small mouth.
Habitat: This fish swims close to the surface of the sea preying on small fish, squids and crustaceans.
Alimentary value: The Mackerel has a very good taste. but its value has decreased because other species such as Tuna and Swordfish have become more popular among Maltese and tourists alike.
Fishing methods: The Atlantic Mackerel is caught by a method that makes use of light (*sajd bil-lampara*). The word *lampara* is derived from *lampa* which emits light. At night a light from a boat attracts many small insects on which the fish can feed. Another boat is then used to haul a net and encircle the gathered fish. Amateur fishing for the Atlantic Mackerel is very different from professional fishing. A light from a boat is still used to attract the fish that is then caught on a shining hook, without bait, as the fish snatches anything that shines.

M: Kelb Abjad
E: Great White Shark
L: Carcharodon carcharias

Size and weight: This monster of the sea reaches a length of about 10m and a weight of about 6000kg.
Characteristics: This shark has a large head and mouth, but its eyes are relatively small. The back is grey and the abdomen is whitish.
Habitat: It lives in deep waters and it is considered to be the most dangerous fish.
Alimentary value and fishing methods: No fisherman will be as courageous to catch this fish.

M: Kelb il-Baħar
E: Tope Shark
L: Galeorhinus galeus

Size and weight: This shark reaches a length of about 2m and a weight of about 34kg.
Characteristics: This shark has a pointed snout and big eyes. It has large fins. The upper lobe of the fish, which is larger than the lower one is notched.
Habitat: It is mostly found in deep waters but it can also swim in coastal waters.
Alimentary value: This shark has a good flesh but many people do not like to buy a shark for dinner!.
Fishing methods: This fish is often caught in trawl nets (*xbieki tat-tkarkir*) and gill nets (*għeżula*). It may also be caught with the surface long-lines (*konzijiet tal-wiċċ*) used to catch the Swordfish and Tuna. Some amateur fishermen venture to catch this fish by using a particular technique. The fisherman holds a rod that is connected to a large buoy from which a metal cable projects vertically towards the sea bed. To this metal cable are tied large hooks that are baited with whole fish.

M: *Kubrita*
E: *Little Tunny*
L: *Euthynnus alletteratus*

Size and weight: This fish reaches a length of just under a metre and a weight of about 6kg.
Characteristics: It is similar to the Frigate Mackerel but it is larger. It can be distinguished from the latter from 6 to 9 small dark spots on its flanks.
Habitat: It lives close to the surface of the sea and eats on small fish.
Alimentary value: The flesh of the Little Tunny is good but dry.
Fishing methods: This fish is caught in nets which however have a larger mesh size then those used for the Frigate Mackerel. Amateur fishermen catch this fish by trolling (*sajd bir-rixa*), similar to that used to catch the Frigate Mackerel.

M: Kurazza Komuni
E: Smooth Hammerhead Shark
L: Sphyrna zygaena

Size and weight: This fish reaches a length of 3m and a weight of about 350kg.
Characteristics: The head of this fish has the shape of a hammer. The fish is grey in colour.
Habitat: It lives in deep waters although it often enters in coastal areas.
Alimentary value: This fish is not sought for its flesh.
Fishing methods: This fish is often caught in trawl nets (*xbieki tat-tkarkir*) and gill nets (*għeżula*). It may also be caught with the surface long-lines (*konzijiet tal-wiċċ*) used to catch the Swordfish and Tuna. Some amateur fishermen venture to catch this fish by using a particular technique. The fisherman holds a rod that is connected to a large buoy from which a metal cable projects vertically towards the sea bed. To this metal cable are tied large hooks that are baited with whole fish.

M: *Kurunella*
E: **Common Sand Smelt**
L: *Atherina hepsetus*

Size and weight: This fish reaches a length of about 10cm and a weight of about 100g.
Characteristics: This is a small silvery fish. It has a dark back that is spotted. Another similar species is the Big-scaled Sand Smelt.
Habitat: This fish lives in shallow coastal waters.
Alimentary value: The Sand Smelt, together with the Transparent Goby, is used to make fish cakes (*pulpetti*).
Fishing methods: A fine cast net (*terrieha*) is used to catch the Sand Smelt. This consists of a net attached to a round metal frame. Sometimes it is also caught on a small hook.

M: *Lacċa Kaħla*
E: *Sprat*
L: *Sprattus sprattus*

Size and weight: It reaches a length of about 15cm and a weight of about 100g.
Characteristics: This fish has a blue-green back and silvery flanks.
Habitat: It lives close to shallow coastal waters.
Alimentary value: This is very low.
Fishing methods: This is caught by the use of fishing rods or inside nets.

M: *Laċċa tat-Tbajja*
E: *Mediterranean Twaite Shad*
L: *Alosa fallax*

Size and weight: This reaches a length of about 50cm and a weight of 1.5kg.
Characteristics: The Shad has a blue-green back and silver flanks. It has about seven horizontal blotches along the upper side of its flanks.
Habitat: It lives close to the coast but it is found in large numbers in the open sea.
Alimentary value: The Shad is often preserved in cans.
Fishing methods: It can be caught by the use of the rod but larger numbers are caught in nets such as the trammel nets (*pariti*), gill nets (*xketti*) and seine nets (*tartaruni*).

M: Lampuka
E: Dolphin Fish, Dorado,
Coryphaene
L: Coryphaena hippurus

Size and weight: The Dolphin Fish can reach a length of about 1.5m and a weight of about 40kg.

Characteristics: This is an elongated and flattened fish. The male has a steeper forehead than the female. This fish has beautiful colours. Its back is blue. On its flanks there are green, yellow and golden colours. The alternative name Dorado is derived from this latter colour.

Habitat: This fish swims near the surface in the open sea. It eats on small fish.

Alimentary value: This fish has a very good flesh and is most common between September and December.

Fishing methods: Amateur fishermen catch the Dolphin Fish by trolling (*sajd bir-rixa*). The most popular type of fishing for this fish makes use of floats (*kannizzata*). It is believed that this fish shelters under anything that floats to defend itself from Dolphins. By time, throughout the ages, fishermen noticed this habit and started attaching palm fronds to the floats to increase the shelter provided, as well as to provide this fish with food as it tends to nibble grass that grows on the fronds. When a good number of fish gather under the float, these are encircled by a net. When the sea is rough, the surface long-line (*konz tal-wiċċ*) may be used.

M: Lhudi
E: Peacock Wrasse
L: Thalassoma pavo

Size and weight: The Wrasse reaches a length of about 20cm and a weight of about 100g.
Characteristics: This is one of the most colourful fish. It has various colours including red, green and orange on its head, as well as blue and orange stripes on its flanks. The female fish is smaller and less colourful.
Habitat: The Peacock Wrasse is found close to the shore in shallow waters.
Alimentary value: The flesh of this fish is good and is used for fish stock.
Fishing methods: This is not commonly caught by fishermen, but it can be caught by the use of a fishing rod as well as long-lines which are attached to a sail (*mrejkba*).

M: Lingwata Komuni
E: Common Sole
L: Solea solea

Size and weight: The Common Sole reaches a length of about 30cm and a weight of about 200g.
Characteristics: The Sole is oval in shape and flat, often referred to as the shape of a tongue. Its eyes are on the right side of its body. It has a greyish-brown colour. Other species include the Yellow Sole, the Thick-back Sole, the Whiskered Sole, the Four-eyed Sole, the Adriatic Sole and the Klein's Sole.
Habitat: This fish lives on sandy sea beds.
Alimentary value: The Sole has a delicious flesh but it is not commonly found in the housewife's menu.
Fishing methods: It is caught in trammel nets (*pariti*) and trawl nets (*xbieki tat-tkarkir*), mostly on sandy bottoms.

M: Lingwata Lixxa
E: Scaldfish
L: Arnoglossus laterna

Size and weight: The Scaldfish reaches a length of up to 20cm and a weight of about 100g.
Characteristics: This fish has an oval and flat body. Both eyes are close to each other on the left side of the body. It has a pale brown colour with darker spots on the left side of its body. The right side of the body is pale. It has big scales that tear off easily as if scalded, hence the name.
Habitat: This fish lives on sandy sea beds.
Alimentary value: The Scaldfish has a delicious flesh but it is not commonly found in the housewife's menu.
Fishing methods: It is caught in trammel nets (*pariti*) and trawl nets (*xbieki tat-tkarkir*), mostly on sandy bottoms.

M: *Lingwata ta' l-Iskwami*
E: *Spotted Flounder*
L: *Citharus linguatula*

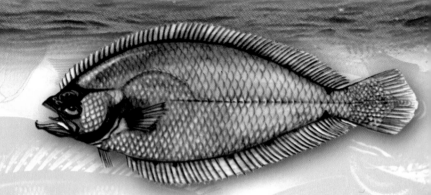

Size and weight: This fish reaches a length of about 30cm and a weight of about 200g.
Characteristics: This fish has an oval and flat body. Its eyes are both on the left of the body close to each other. It has a pale yellowish-brown colour with darker spots close to the head. The right side of the body is whitish. This fish has large scales. It has two dark spots just before the tail.
Habitat: This fish lives on sandy sea beds.
Alimentary value: The fish has a delicious flesh but it is not commonly found in the housewife's menu.
Fishing methods: It is caught in trammel nets (*pariti*) and trawl nets (*xbieki tat-tkarkir*), mostly on sandy bottoms.

M: *Lipp Abjad*
E: *Forkbeard*
L: *Phycis blennoides*

Size and weight: This fish can reach a length of 60cm and a weight of about 3kg.
Characteristics: This fish has a longitudinal shape. The lower jaw is shorter than the upper one and has a protruding single short barbel. The back of this Forkbeard is brown and the flanks are silvery.
Habitat: This fish lives close to the surface of the open sea.
Alimentary value: This fish is not of any particular alimentary value.
Fishing methods: The Greater Forkbeard is caught in nets.

M: Lizz
E: Mediterranean Barracuda
L: Sphyraena sphyraena

Size and weight: The Barracuda reaches a length of about 1.2m and a weight of about 10kg.
Characteristics: The Barracuda has an elongated body tapering at both ends. The jaws possess strong pointed teeth. Underwater fishermen are afraid of this fish as it has occasionally attacked people. The Barracuda has a grey back with olive-green reflections and numerous dark vertical bands running down the silvery sides, and is pale underneath.
Habitat: This fish is migratory and it is found in open waters as well as in shallow waters.
Alimentary value: The Barracuda has a good flesh.
Fishing methods: The European Barracuda is caught in trammel nets (*pariti*) and gill nets (*xketti*). The fish is caught by amateur fishermen mostly at dawn and dask. The most common method is by trawling (*sajd bir-rixa*) with artificial lures. It also offers a challenge to underwater fishermen.

M: *Makku*
E: *Transparent Goby*
L: *Aphia minuta*

Size and weight: This small fish reaches a length of about 5cm and a weight of about 5g.
Characteristics: This is a small elongated fish. Its eyes are relatively big. Its skin is transparent.
Habitat: The Goby lives in shallow coastal waters.
Alimentary value: It is used to make fish cakes.
Fishing methods: The cast net (*terrieħa*), a net with fine mesh attached to a circular metal frame, is used to catch the Goby.

M: Marlozz
E: European Hake
L: Merluccus merluccus

Size and weight: This fish grows up to a length of 1m and a weight of up to 7kg.
Characteristics: The Hake has an elongated body and a big head. Its back is grey and its abdomen is pale.
Habitat: It lives close to the sea bed, but in summer it reaches shallower waters.
Alimentary value: It has a good flesh and its liver is rich in vitamins.
Fishing methods: The Hake is caught in nets. It is also caught by bottom long-lines or by underwater fishing.

M: Marżpan, Pappagall Ahmar
E: Red Parrotfish
L: Sparisoma cretense

Size and weight: This fish grows up to 50cm in length and a weight of 1.5kg.
Characteristics: This is a beautiful fish. It has an oval body with a small mouth and jaws resembling the beak of a parrot. The eyes are small. The male is coloured grey all over except for a dark blotch behind the gill operculum. Females are smaller and red in colour with an extensive grey area behind the eyes and over the pectoral fins, and yellow markings behind the eyes and the top of the tail stalk.
Habitat: The Parrotfish lives close to rocky sea beds and coral reefs.
Alimentary value: Its flesh is not very good.
Fishing methods: The Parrotfish is most commonly caught by the fishing rod or by underwater fishing.

M: Marżpan, Pappagall Griż
E: Grey Parrotfish
L: Sparisoma cretense

Size and weight: This fish grows up to 50cm in length and a weight of 1.5kg.
Characteristics: This is a beautiful fish. It has an oval body with a small mouth and jaws resembling the beak of a parrot. The eyes are small. The male is coloured grey all over except for a dark blotch behind the gill operculum. Females are smaller and red in colour with an extensive grey area behind the eyes and over the pectoral fins, and yellow markings behind the eyes and the top of the tail stalk.
Habitat: The Parrotfish lives close to rocky sea beds and coral reefs.
Alimentary value: Its flesh is not very good.
Fishing methods: The Parrotfish is most commonly caught by the fishing rod or by underwater fishing.

M: *Mazzola bla Xewka*
E: **Smooth Hound**
L: **Mustelus mustelus**

Size and weight: This grows to a length of about 1m and a weight of about 20kg.
Characteristics: It has an elongated body with a notched upper tail lobe.
Habitat: The Smooth Hound lives close to the sea bed. Other species include Longnose Spurdog, Starry Smooth Hound and Spur.
Alimentary value: This is still a popular edible fish, but Tuna and Swordfish are still preferred.
Fishing methods: The Smooth Hound is caught by bottom long-lines (*konz tal-pistin*). A typical long-line may be about 2km long with about 500 baited hooks. Fishermen claim that the most important factor is not the technique but the place where to haul the long-line. Long nets, which are allowed to drift along the sea bed, are also used to catch this bottom dwelling fish. Only a few amateur fishermen have the necessary vessels and fishing tackle for catching this fish. Reels can be used having strong nylon lines and large hooks baited with pieces of fish. A heavy weight is necessary to sink the bait to the sea bed.

M: *Mazzola Griża*
E: *Spurdog, Piked Dogfish*
L: *Squalus acanthias*

Size and weight: This grows to a length of about 1m and a weight of about 20kg.
Characteristics: The Spur is grey in colour with a pale abdomen.
Habitat: The Spur lives close to the sea bed.
Alimentary value: This is still a popular edible fish but Tuna and Swordfish are still preferred.
Fishing methods: The Spur is caught by bottom long-lines (*konz tal-pistin*). A typical long-line may be about 2km long with about 500 baited hooks. Fishermen claim that the most important factor is not the technique but the place where to haul the long-line. Long nets that are allowed to drift along the sea bed are also used to catch this bottom dwelling fish. Only a few amateur fishermen have the necessary vessels and fishing tackle for catching this fish. Reels can be used having strong nylon lines and large hooks baited with pieces of fish. A heavy weight is necessary to sink the bait to the sea bed.

M: Mazzun Iswed
E: Black Goby
L: Gobius niger

Size and weight: This grows up to 10cm and a weight of about 70g.
Characteristics: This is a small fish and the colour depends on the species. These include Slender Goby, Bucchich's Goby, Giant Goby, Red-mouthed Goby, Rock Goby, Sand Goby and Grass Goby.
Habitat: The Goby lives on rocky bottoms and swallows anything that passes by.
Alimentary value: This is not an edible fish.
Fishing methods: This is usually conducted at night. A line can be hauled from the boat (*mitlaq*) or else a rod with reel can be used from the coast.

M: *Merlin*
E: *Green Wrasse*
L: *Labrus viridis*

Size and weight: This fish grows a length of about 45cm and reaches a weight of about 1.2kg.
Characteristics: The Green Wrasse has an elongated body and has large lips. It has beautiful colours and two varieties exist. The red variety has tinges of brown or orange reflections, with an abundant number of small, pale spots. The green variety has olive shades with a reddish hue on the gill covers and abdomen.
Habitat: The Green Wrasse lives close to shallow rocky bottoms.
Alimentary value: It is mostly used to prepare fish stock.
Fishing methods: The amateur fisherman catches this fish by use of the fishing rod or by underwater fishing. It is also caught from the boat by hauling a line (*mitlaq*) with a small hook baited with shrimps or snails.

M: Minfah, Bassas
E: Boarfish
L: Capros aper

Size and weight: The Boarfish grows up to 15cm in length and reaches a weight of about 120g.
Characteristics: This fish has a wide and flat body. It has big eyes. In deep waters it has a reddish colour but in shallow waters it obtains a pale straw colour.
Habitat: It lives mostly close to the sea bed in deep waters.
Alimentary value: The Boarfish has a good flesh which is not much appreciated.
Fishing methods: It is caught in trawl nets (*xbieki tat-tkarkir*) and sometimes on lines cast from boats (*mitlaq*).

M: Mingus
E: Marmora, Striped Sea Bream
L: Lithognathus mormyrus

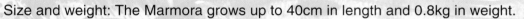

Size and weight: The Marmora grows up to 40cm in length and 0.8kg in weight.
Characteristics: The fish has an elongated body and a big head. Its colour is silvery-white, darker above, with up to fifteen dark vertical stripes on its flanks. It is almost white underside.
Habitat: This fish lives in shallow waters on sand and muddy bottoms.
Alimentary value: The Marmora has a good flesh that is not much appreciated.
Fishing methods: The Marmora is caught by the use of a fishing rod.

M: *Morina*
E: *Moray Eel*
L: *Muraena helena*

Size and weight: This fish grows more than a metre in length and reaches a weight of about 10kg.
Characteristics: The Eel is dark brown in colour, with yellow patches. It has a serpentine shape. It has powerful jaws with pointed teeth. It eats mostly at night when it peeps out of crevices in rocks to eat on small fish or the tentacle of an octopus.
Habitat: It lives in rocky crevices and grassy bottoms.
Alimentary value: The meat of the Moray Eel is edible but is packed with long, thin and sharp spines which are most annoying to remove. The serpent-like shape seems to prevent some housewives from including it in the weekly home menu.
Fishing methods: The Eel is mostly caught with bottom long-lines (*konz tal-qiegh*). Its powerful jaw and teeth can easily cut the line and so a piece of metal wire should be used with the hook. Pieces of fish and octopus may be used as bait. Traps made of metal mesh (*barrada*) may be used to trap the Moray Eel. Underwater fishermen can catch the Eel with the harpoon.

M: Mulett Buri
E: Leaping Grey Mullet
L: Liza saliens

Size and weight: The Grey Mullet grows up to 30cm in length and a weight of up to 1kg.
Characteristics: This Mullet has smaller lips than those of the Thick-lipped Grey Mullet. Its back is dark grey, which gradually fades down to a silvery underside. It has a few dark longitudinal lines on the sides.
Habitat: The Mullet lives in shallow coastal waters and aggregates in small schools inside harbours and bays even if heavily polluted with sewage and oil. It nibbles at weeds and bottom detritus for decomposing vegetable matter and tiny organisms living there.
Alimentary value: The intestines of the Mullet are full of mud and so the housewife often regards this fish as inedible. Its meat, however, is good.
Fishing methods: Pieces of bread soaked with cheese and pieces of meat are used to attract the Mullet to the site. The method makes use of bread that has the form of a snail. This is soaked in water until it grows in size after which it is squeezed and left to dry in a towel. When the bread is opened, strings of bread can be seen. These strings are then soaked in anisette and hooked. A fishing rod or reel is used. Another method makes use of a float to which hooks are attacked (*forka*). A bread roll may also be used; hooks attached to a common line are wound around the bread roll that is thrown on the surface of the sea with a rod mounted with a reel. While the Mullet gulps the bread, the fisherman hopes that it swallows one of the hooks.

M: *Mulett Kaplat*
E: *Thick-lipped Grey Mullet*
L: *Chelon labrosus*

Size and weight: This fish grows up to 80cm in length and a weight of about 2kg.
Characteristics: This is an elongated fish with thick lips. It has a bluish-grey back, metallic flanks and a white abdomen.
Habitat: The Mullet lives in shallow coastal waters and aggregates in small schools inside harbours and bays even if heavily polluted with sewage and oil. It nibbles at weeds and bottom detritus for decomposing vegetable matter and tiny organisms living there.
Alimentary value: The intestines of the Mullet are full of mud and so the housewife often regards this fish as inedible. Its meat, however, is good.
Fishing methods: Pieces of bread soaked with cheese and pieces of meat are used to attract the Mullet to the site. The method makes use of bread that has the form of a snail. This is soaked in water until it grows in size after which it is squeezed and left to dry in a towel. When the bread is opened, strings of bread can be seen. These strings are then soaked in anisette and hooked. A fishing rod or reel is used. Another method makes use of a float to which hooks are attacked (*forka*). A bread roll may also be used; hooks attached to a common line are wound around the bread roll that is thrown on the surface of the sea with a rod mounted with a reel. While the Mullet gulps the bread, the fisherman hopes that it swallows one of the hooks.

M: Mulett taċ-Ċarruta Safra
E: Golden Mullet
L: Liza aurata

Size and weight: This fish grows up to a length of about 40cm and a weight of about 1kg.

Characteristics: This species of Mullet is recognized from the other species from its colour. It has a golden blotch on each gill cover. It has thin lips.

Habitat: The Mullet lives in shallow coastal waters and aggregates in small schools inside harbours and bays even if heavily polluted with sewage and oil. It nibbles at weeds and bottom detritus for decomposing vegetable matter and tiny organisms living there.

Alimentary value: The intestines of the Mullet are full of mud and so the housewife often regards this fish as inedible. Its meat, however, is good.

Fishing methods: Pieces of bread soaked with cheese and pieces of meat are used to attract the Mullet to the site. The method makes use of bread that has the form of a snail. This is soaked in water until it grows in size after which it is squeezed and left to dry in a towel. When the bread is opened, strings of bread can be seen. These strings are then soaked in anisette and hooked. A fishing rod or reel is used. Another method makes use of a float to which hooks are attacked (*forka*). A bread roll may also be used; hooks attached to a common line are wound around the bread roll that is thrown on the surface of the sea with a rod mounted with a reel. While the Mullet gulps the bread, the fisherman hopes that it swallows one of the hooks.

M: *Mulett ta' l-Imċarrat*
E: **Thin-lipped Grey Mullet**
L.: *Liza ramada*

Size and weight: This Mullet reaches a size of about 60cm and a weight of about 1.5kg.

Characteristics: It has a brownish back and its flanks are silvery-blue. The abdomen is pale.

Habitat: The Mullet lives in shallow coastal waters and aggregates in small schools inside harbours and bays even if heavily polluted with sewage and oil. It nibbles at weeds and bottom detritus for decomposing vegetable matter and tiny organisms living there.

Alimentary value: The intestines of the Mullet are full of mud and so the housewife often regards this fish as inedible. Its meat, however, is good.

Fishing methods: Pieces of bread soaked with cheese and pieces of meat are used to attract the Mullet to the site. The method makes use of bread that has the form of a snail. This is soaked in water until it grows in size after which it is squeezed and left to dry in a towel. When the bread is opened, strings of bread can be seen. These strings are then soaked in anisette and hooked. A fishing rod or reel is used. Another method makes use of a float to which hooks are attached (*forka*). A bread roll may also be used; hooks attached to a common line are wound around the bread roll that is thrown on the surface of the sea with a rod mounted with a reel. While the Mullet gulps the bread, the fisherman hopes that it swallows one of the hooks.

M: *Mulett ta' l-Iswed*
E: **Striped Mullet**
L: **Mugil cephalus**

Size and weight: This Mullet grows up to 80cm in length and 2kg in weight.

Characteristics: This Mullet has thin lips. Its back is greenish or dark blue. Its flanks are silvery-grey and have dark grey parallel lines joining the pectoral fin area to the tail peduncle.

Habitat: The Mullet lives in shallow coastal waters and aggregates in small schools inside harbours and bays even if heavily polluted with sewage and oil. It nibbles at weeds and bottom detritus for decomposing vegetable matter and tiny organisms living there.

Alimentary value: The intestines of the Mullet are full of mud and so the housewife often regards this fish as inedible. Its meat, however, is good.

Fishing methods: Pieces of bread soaked with cheese and pieces of meat are used to attract the Mullet to the site. The method makes use of bread that has the form of a snail. This is soaked in water until it grows in size after which it is squeezed and left to dry in a towel. When the bread is opened, strings of bread can be seen. These strings are then soaked in anisette and hooked. A fishing rod or reel is used. Another method makes use of a float to which hooks are attached (*forka*). A bread roll may also be used; hooks attached to a common line are wound around the bread roll that is thrown on the surface of the sea with a rod mounted with a reel. While the Mullet gulps the bread, the fisherman hopes that it swallows one of the hooks.

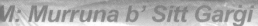

M: *Murruna b' Sitt Gargi*
E: **Sixgill Shark**
L: *Hexanchus griseus*

Size and weight: This shark grows up to 5m in length and 200kg in weight.
Characteristics: The fish has a short blunt snout. It has relatively small eyes. The upper lobe of its tail is much longer than the lower one. The back of the shark is grey or dark brown, and its abdomen is pale. Another similar species is the Sharpnose Sevengill Shark.
Habitat: It lives in deep waters but it often enters coastal waters.
Alimentary value: This shark has a good flesh but many people do not like to buy a shark for dinner!
Fishing methods: This fish is often caught in trawl nets (*xbieki tat-tkarkir*) and gill nets (*għeżula*). It may also be caught with the surface long-lines (*konzijiet tal-wiċċ*) used to catch the swordfish and tuna. Some amateur fishermen venture to catch this fish by using a particular technique. The fisherman holds a rod that is connected to a large buoy from which a metal cable projects vertically towards the sea bed. To this metal cable are tied large hooks that are baited with whole fish.

M: Pagella Hamra
E: Pandora
L: Pagellus erythrinus

Size and weight: The Pandora can grow to a length of about 50cm and a weight of about 2kg.
Characteristics: The fish has an oval body. It has a reddish-pink colour.
Habitat: The Pandora lives close to sandy sea beds between 20 and 300m deep.
Alimentary value: The flesh of this fish is tender and delicious.
Fishing methods: The Pandora is often caught in trawl nets (*xbieki tat-tkarkir*) and trammel nets (*pariti*). The amateur fisherman catches the Pandora by the bottom line (*mitlaq*) from a boat. The line diameter should be of 0.40mm and a hook size 4 should be used. Shrimps and worms are preferred baits. While hauling in a Pandora it often happens that the fish swims upward along the line giving the impression that it freed itself from the hook. The fisherman is however soon reassured when it dives downwards once more.

M: *Pagella tal-Gargi*

E: *Red Sea Bream,*
   Black Spot Sea Bream

L: *Pagellus bogaraveo*

Size and weight: The Red Sea Bream can grow to a length of about 80cm and a weight of about 3kg.
Characteristics: The fish has an oval body. It has a reddish-pink colour with a distinctive black patch just behind the neck.
Habitat: The Red Sea Bream lives close to sandy sea beds between 20 and 300m deep.
Alimentary value: The flesh of this fish is tender and delicious.
Fishing methods: The Red Sea Bream is often caught in trawl nets (*xbieki tat-tkarkir*) and trammel nets (*pariti*). The amateur fisherman catches the Bream by the bottom line (*mitlaq*) from a boat. The line diameter should be of 0.40mm and a hook size 4 should be used. Shrimps and worms are preferred baits. While hauling in a Red Sea Bream it often happens that the fish swims upward along the line giving the impression that it freed itself from the hook. The fisherman is however soon reassured when it dives downwards once more.

M: Pagru Komuni
E: Couch's Sea Bream
L: Pagrus pagrus

Size and weight: The fish grows up to 80cm in length and 4kg in weight.
Characteristics: This fish has an oval body with a slight bump in front of its eyes. This latter characteristic can distinguish it from the Pandora. Its back is dark but the flanks are pink with some small blue spots.
Habitat: This fish lives close to the sea bed but not only on sandy bottoms.
Alimentary value: The flesh of the Couch's Sea Bream is very good.
Fishing methods: This fish is caught in nets and bottom long-lines (*konzijiet tal-qiegh*) on reefs. The fish can also be caught with the bottom line (*mitlaq*) hauled from a boat.

M: Pagru Rar
E: Blue-Spotted Sea Bream
L: Pagrus coerulostrictus

Size and weight: The fish grows up to 50cm in length and 2kg in weight.
Characteristics: This fish has an oval body. Its back is dark but the flanks are pink with blue spots that distinguish it from the Couch's Sea Bream. It also lacks the bump in front of its eyes.
Habitat: This fish lives close to the sea bed but not only on sandy bottoms.
Alimentary value: The flesh of the Blue-spotted Sea Bream is very good.
Fishing methods: This fish is caught in nets and bottom long-lines (*konzijiet tal-qiegħ*) on reefs. The fish can also be caught with the bottom line (*mitlaq*) hauled from a boat.

M: *Parpanjol*
E: Cuckoo Wrasse
L: Labrus bimaculatus

Size and weight: This fish grows a length of about 30cm and a weight of about 300g.
Characteristics: The Cuckoo Wrasse is an elongated fish. The male has blue, orange and yellow colours. The female has an orange-red colour but has up to four brown or black blotches on the back and tail peduncle.
Habitat: This Wrasse lives close to the sea bed.
Alimentary value: The fish is mostly used for fish stock.
Fishing methods: It is mostly caught by the bottom line (*mitlaq*) or by the harpoon.

M: **Pastardella**
E: **Spearfish**
L: *Tetrapturus pfluegeri*

Size and weight: This fish grows up to a length of about 2m and a weight of about 50kg.
Characteristics: The fish is elongated and tapering to a bill at the front. It resembles the Swordfish but has a flatter body.
Habitat: The Spearfish lives close to the surface in open seas.
Alimentary value: Its flesh is good although it is not as popular as the Swordfish.
Fishing methods: The Mediterranean Spearfish is caught by the surface long-line (*konz tal-wiċċ*) used to catch the Swordfish. It is also caught by trolling (*sajd bir-rixa*) with Mackerel and Scad, preferably still alive. The fish is on the decrease as young immature species are being caught.

M: *Petrica*
E: *Anglerfish*
L: *Lophius piscatorius*

Size and weight: This fish can grow up to a length of about 1.5m and a weight of about 15kg.
Characteristics: The Anglerfish has a large mouth. It has a flat body. It is brown in colour.
Habitat: It lives on sandy bottoms where it can hide under the sand.
Alimentary value: The head of this fish comprises the larger part of the body, but its tail end is edible.
Fishing methods: The Anglerfish is caught in nets, especially trawl nets (*xbieki tat-tkarkir*). It could also be caught in bottom long-lines (*konzijiet tal-qiegh*).

M: *Pixxi Luna*
E: **Ray's Bream, Bulleye**
L: *Brama brama*

Size and weight: The Bulleye can grow up to a length of about 70cm and a weight of about 13kg.
Characteristics: The Bulleye has a laterally compressed oval body. It has a big head and prominent circular eyes. Its back is dark brown that becomes paler over the flanks.
Habitat: It lives in high seas but is found in mid-waters.
Alimentary value: This is not a popular fish in our islands but it is considered to be of great alimentary value in other countries.
Fishing methods: The Bulleye is caught in long-lines (*konzijiet*) and nets.

M: Pixxiplamtu
E: Porbeagle Shark
L: Lamna nasus

Size and weight: This shark can grow up to a length of about 3.5m and a weight of about 500kg.
Characteristics: This fish has a robust body. It has a dark coloured back but is pale underside.
Habitat: This shark lives in the open sea and swims at the surface, sometimes approaching coasts.
Alimentary value: This shark is of little alimentary value.
Fishing methods: This fish is often caught in trawl nets (*xbieki tat-tkarkir*) and gill nets (*għeżula*). It may also be caught with the surface long-lines (*konzijiet tal-wiċċ*) used to catch the swordfish and tuna. Some amateur fishermen venture to catch this fish by using a particular technique. The fisherman holds a rod that is connected to a large buoy from which a metal cable projects vertically towards the sea bed. To this metal cable are tied large hooks that are baited with whole fish.

M: *Pixxi San Pietru*

E: **John Dory**

L: *Zeus faber*

Size and weight: This fish reaches a length of about 50cm and a weight of about 400g.

Characteristics: The John Dory has a deep and flattened body. It has a big head with prominent eyes. It has long spines on its back. The fish has a grey colour with a black spot on each side. Tradition holds that this spot was caused by the fingers of St Peter who collected tribute money from the mouth of the John Dory.

Habitat: The fish lives in shallow and deep waters alike.

Alimentary value: The flesh of this fish is very good.

Fishing Methods: The John Dory is caught in fishing nets and bottom long-lines (*konzijiet tal-qiegh*). It is caught by amateur fishermen with the use of the harpoon and bottom line (*mitlaq*).

M: Pixxispad
E: *Swordfish*
L: *Xiphias gladius*

Size and weight: The Swordfish can grow up to 5m in length and 500kg in weight.
Characteristics: This fish has a large mouth and an elongated rostrum protruding for a metre or so. It has an elongated body and wide tail which allows it to swim fast. It eats on smaller fish that it kills with its sword.
Habitat: The Swordfish swims close to the surface but can venture down to several metres when the sea becomes cold. This fish migrates over long distances.
Alimentary value: This fish has a very important market value and has gained popularity over the years.
Fishing methods: The Swordfish is caught by the surface long-line (*konz tal-wiċċ*). This was first used in Malta in 1953. This long-line is usually made of kilometres of nylon. Between each hook there is usually a distance of about 60 metres. Between 100 and 300 hooks are used and Scad and Mackerel are used as bait. In Gozo the long-line is also used, but this is tied to weights in such a way that the line is 1 metre below the surface of the sea (*ormeġġi*). Amateur fishermen may use strong rods with reels that are strong enough to withstand the struggle that this fish offers when caught.

M: *Pixxifondu*
E: **Shortfin Mako**
L: *Isurus oxyrinchus*

Size and weight: This fish reaches a length of about 4m and a weight of about 600kg.
Characteristics: This shark has relatively prominent eyes. Its back is dark blue in colour which changes to a lighter blue on the flanks.
Habitat: It dwells close to the surface far out in the open sea. It is common and may be dangerous.
Alimentary value: This shark is of little alimentary value.
Fishing methods: The Porbeagle fish is often caught in trawl nets (*xbieki tat-tkarkir*) and gill nets (*għeżula*). It may also be caught with the surface long-lines (*konzijiet tal-wiċċ*) used to catch the Swordfish and Tuna. Some amateur fishermen venture to catch this fish by using a particular technique. The fisherman holds a rod that is connected to a large buoy from which a metal cable projects vertically towards the sea bed. To this metal cable are tied large hooks that are baited with whole fish.

M: Pixxivolpi
E: Thresher Shark
L: Alopias vulpinus

Size and weight: This shark can grow up to a length of about 4m and a weight of about 420kg.
Characteristics: The upper lobe of the tail is as long as the rest of the body. Its back is dark green and its abdomen is whitish.
Habitat: This shark lives in the open sea and swims at the surface, sometimes approaching coasts.
Alimentary value: This shark is of little alimentary value.
Fishing methods: This fish is often caught in trawl nets (*xbieki tat-tkarkir*) and gill nets (*għeżula*). It may also be caught with the surface long-lines (*konzijiet tal-wiċċ*) used to catch the swordfish and tuna. Some amateur fishermen venture to catch this fish by using a particular technique. The fisherman holds a rod that is connected to a large buoy from which a metal cable projects vertically towards the sea bed. To this metal cable are tied large hooks that are baited with whole fish.

M: *Plamtu*
E: *Atlantic Bonito*
L: *Sarda sarda*

Size and weight: This fish can grow up to a length of 1m and a weight of about 9kg.

Characteristics: The Bonito is recognized by about 9 oblique black stripes on its flanks. The colour of the back is greenish and a dark blue. There is another species of Bonito that does not have these stripes.

Habitat: The fish migrates close to the surface or in mid-waters.

Alimentary value: The fish has a good taste although some people complain that it is dry.

Fishing methods: It is caught by the amateur fishermen while trolling (*sajd bir-rixa*). This fish offers much resistance and that is why the amateur fisherman is delighted when he catches one. The Atlantic Bonito is also caught in nets.

Since this fish lives close to the bottom, it is caught by underwater fishing. This fish is also caught with bottom long-lines (*konzijiet tal-qiegħ*).

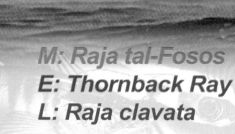

M: *Raja tal-Fosos*
E: Thornback Ray
L: *Raja clavata*

Size and weight: This fish can reach a length of about 1.5m and a weight of about 10kg.
Characteristics: This is a flat fish with a long tail. The eyes are on the upper part of the body, while the gill openings are below.
Habitat: The Thornback Ray lives close to sandy bottoms.
Alimentary value: This is very low.
Fishing methods: Since this fish lives close to the bottom, it is caught by underwater fishing. This fish is also caught with bottom long-lines (*konzijiet tal-qiegh*).

M: *Raja tal- Kwiekeb*
E: *Starry Ray*
L: *Raja asterias*

Size and weight: This fish can grow up to 1m in length and a weight of about 7kg.
Characteristics: It is variably coloured in shades of yellow, brown or green, with circles of spots around white patches.
Habitat: The Starry Ray lives close to the bottom of shallow or deep waters. It is often found covered with sand, waiting to gulp a small fish, a shrimp or a crab.
Alimentary value: The flesh of this fish is very good.
Fishing methods: Amateur fishermen often catch this fish with a harpoon. It is also caught by professional fishermen in trawl nets (*xbieki tat-tkarkir*).

M: Raja tat-Tikek
E: Spotted Ray
L: Raja montagui

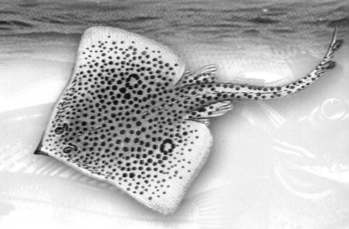

Size and weight: This fish can grow up to 1m in length and a weight of about 7kg.

Characteristics: This is a flat fish with a long tail. The eyes are on the upper part of the body, while the gill openings are below. They have a brownish-green colour with grey areas.

Habitat: This fish lives close to the bottom of shallow or deep waters. It is often found covered with sand, waiting to gulp a small fish, a shrimp or a crab.

Alimentary value: The flesh of this fish is very good.

Fishing methods: Amateur fishermen often catch this fish with a harpoon. It is also caught by professional fishermen in trawl nets (*xbieki tat-tkarkir*).

M: *Rondinella Komuni*
E: **Flying Fish**
L: *Chielopogon heterurus*

Size and weight: This fish can grow up to about 40cm in length and a weight of about 1.5kg.
Characteristics: The flying fish has an elongated body with winged pectoral fins which allow it to fly for a few metres above the surface of the sea. It has a dark blue back with silvery flanks.
Habitat: This fish lives close to the surface of sea water especially in summer and autumn.
Alimentary value: This is very low.
Fishing methods: Fishermen do not usually fish for the Flying Fish however it is caught in nets or while trolling (*sajd bir-rixa*).

M: Rużetta
E: Cleaver Wrasse
L: Xyrichthys novacula

Size and weight: This fish can grow up to 40cm in length and a weight of about 1.5kg.

Characteristics: It has a reddish-pink colour with silvery stripes on its flanks. The male fish has a stronger reddish colour that can have a greenish shade.

Habitat: This fish lives on sandy bottoms in depths of between 10 and 100m.

Alimentary value: The flesh of this fish is very good and some people prefer it from the flesh of the Red Mullet.

Fishing methods: The amateur fishermen can spend a happy hour if he knows the right place where to find this fish. The best way to catch it is by the use of the bottom line (mitlaq). The first hook should be close to the weight, for example 5cm. If present in good numbers, the Wrasse could be easily caught in large numbers and in a short time. It is important to use a cloth to handle the fish, as it is very slippery. The fishermen should be careful as the fish has a tendency to bite. It is best to use small pliers in order to remove the hook from the fish's mouth. The best bait is pieces of shrimps or snails.

M: Sallura
E: Common European Eel
L: Anguilla anguilla

Size and weight: The fish can grow up to 1m in length and a weight of about 3kg.
Characteristics: The Eel has a serpentine body. It has a greyish black colour.
Habitat: This fish can live in both salty and fresh water. It lives mostly in muddy inlets. It is often placed in wells in order to eat any organisms that live in the fresh water.
Alimentary value: Many people do not like to cook this fish, mostly because of its serpentine shape.
Fishing methods: It can be caught with bottom long-lines (*konzijiet tal-qiegħ*). Metal wires should be used because this fish can easily bite a nylon line with its teeth. Various types of bait can be used, such as pieces of fish, shrimps and crabs. The Eels may be caught in traps made of metal mesh, like those used to catch the Conger and Moray Eels.

M: Sardina Hadra
E: European Pilchard, Sardine
L: Sardina pilchardus

Size and weight: This fish grows to a length of about 20cm and a weight of about 200g.
Characteristics: The back has a dark olive-green colour and silvery sides.
Habitat: This fish is encountered inside harbours and bays.
Alimentary value: The fish is exploited by the preservative industry.
Fishing methods: It is mostly caught in nets.

M: *Sargu Komuni*
E: **White Sea Bream**
L: *Diplodus sargus*

Size and weight: The fish can grow up to a length of about 30cm and a weight of about 1.5kg.
Characteristics: It has an ovoid body, a large head and thick lips. It has a silver colour with seven black bands running down its flanks. The Bream has a black blotch on the tail stalk. It eats crustaceans, shrimps, sea urchins and small fish.
Habitat: This fish is found in shoals of 10 to 100 members, near rocky bottoms.
Alimentary value: The flesh of this fish is very good.
Fishing methods: The most popular time to fish for the White Sea Bream is between May and November. The line must be at least 0.25mm in diameter with a hook size 8. The smaller specimens are found near to the coast close to the sea bed, however during sunset, the larger specimens swim closer to the shore looking for food. The fish is easily caught during underwater fishing. The illegal use of explosives is killing a lot of White Sea Bream. Fishing nets such as the trammel net (*parit*) are entrapping small specimens that are not left to reproduce.

M: Sawrella Imperjali Denbha Iswed
E: Blue Runner
L: Caranx crysos

Size and weight: This fish can reach a length of about 50cm and a weight of about 4kg.
Characteristics: The Blue Runner is slightly different from the European Scad as it has a deeper body. Its back is greenish-blue while the flanks are silvery grey. The abdomen is grey.
Habitat: This fish lives close to the surface of the sea and it is very common.
Alimentary value: Its white flesh is tasty and tender and so it is fished for on a commercial basis.
Fishing methods: The Blue Runner is caught by a method that makes use of light (*sajd bil-lampara*). The word *lampara* is derived from *lampa* that emits light. At night a light from a boat attracts many small insects on which the fish can feed. Another boat is then used to haul a net and encircle the gathered fish. Amateur fishing for the Blue Runner is very different from professional fishing. A light from a boat is still used to attract the fish that is then caught on a shining hook without bait as the fish snatches anything that shines.

M: *Sawrella Kaħla*
E: **Horse Mackerel, European Scad**
L: *Trachurus trachurus*

Size and weight: This fish can reach a length of about 40cm and a weight of about 1.2kg.
Characteristics: This is an elongated fish. It has a small black blotch at the base of the operculum. It has a bluish-grey colour with greenish tints. The sides of the fish are silvery and its belly is white.
Habitat: This fish lives close to the surface of the sea and it is very common.
Alimentary value: Its white flesh is tasty and tender and so it is fished for on a commercial basis.
Fishing methods: The European Scad is caught by a method that makes use of light (*sajd bil-lampara*). The word *lampara* is derived from *lampa* that emits light. At night a light from a boat attracts many small insects on which the fish can feed. Another boat is then used to haul a net and encircle the gathered fish. Amateur fishing for the European Scad is very different from professional fishing. A light from a float is still used to attract the fish that is then caught on a shining hook without bait as the fish snatches anything that shines.

M: Sawt
E: Lesser Weever
L: Echiichthys vipera

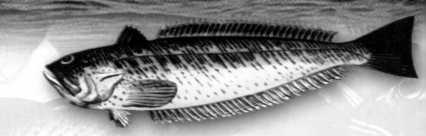

Size and weight: This fish can grow up to a length of about 15cm and a weight of about 150g.
Characteristics: This fish has a large head with small eyes almost on top. It is brownish-yellow in colour with dark patches on the back.
Habitat: The Lesser Weever lives mostly on sandy bottoms where it is often found buried under sand or mud, leaving only its eyes peeping out. When a shrimp or a small fish wonders by, the Weever jumps out of the sand to snatch its prey. If accidentally trodden upon, medical attention must be sought because its fins are poisonous.
Alimentary value: This is of little alimentary value but can be used to make fish stock.
Fishing methods: This is mostly caught from sandy sea beds by the use of the bottom line (*mitlaq*). Pieces of shrimps are used as bait

M: *Serra Tas-Snien*
E: **Bluefish, Elft**
L.: *Pomatomus saltator*

Size and weight: This fish can reach a length of about 80cm and a weight of about 5kg.
Characteristics: This fish has an elongated body with prominent eyes and big jaws. The back is coloured blue-green, fading to silvery sides.
Habitat: This fish lives close to the surface of the sea or in mid-waters.
Alimentary value: The flesh of this fish is good.
Fishing methods: This is mostly caught by trolling (*sajd bir-rixa*) or inside nets.

M: *Serran*
E: *Comber*
L: *Serranus cabrilla*

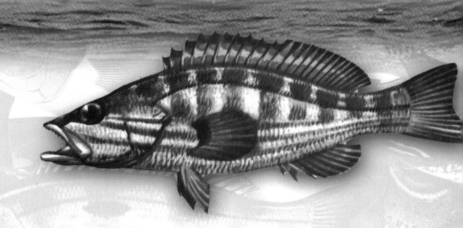

Size and weight: This fish can reach a length of about 30cm and a weight of about 200g.
Characteristics: The Comber has a big mouth and relatively prominent eyes. It is coloured yellowish-brown, with seven to nine dark brown vertical bands on its sides. It has blue-green longitudinal lines along the lower part of the body.
Habitat: The Comber lives close to grassy sea beds. It feeds on small fish or mollusks.
Alimentary value: The Comber has a fine flesh which is usually used to prepare fish stock.
Fishing methods: Since it lives close to the sea bed, the bottom line (*mitlaq*) is the method most commonly practiced by amateur fishermen. Bait includes shrimps, snails and sand hoppers (*ċkal*). Larger specimens can be caught by the use of the harpoon. Reel rods may be used to catch the fish from the coast. Unfortunately the fish dies soon after it is brought to the surface because of the change in pressure. Because of this, if a small specimen is caught and freed, it may not live.

M: *Skalm*
E: *Mediterranean Lizardfish*
L: *Synodus taurus*

Size and weight: This fish grows up to a length of about 30cm and a weight of about 500g.

Characteristics: This elongated fish has a head which resembles that of a lizard. It has shades of brown and olive colours with irregular darker stains. Its abdomen is nearly white.

Habitat: The Lizardfish lives close to sandy sea beds in shallow or deep waters.

Alimentary value: This is very low but it can be used to prepare fish stock.

Fishing methods: This fish is caught in trawl nets (*xbieki tat-tkarkir*) or with bottom long-lines (*konzijiet tal-qiegh*). It is also caught by the bottom line (*mitlaq*) on sandy sea beds and occasionally by trolling (*sajd bir-rixa*) with an artificial lure.

M: Skorfna
E: Scorpionfish
L: Scorpaena notata

Size and weight: This fish grows up to a length of about 20cm and a weight of about 100g.
Characteristics: The fish has a deep body and a relatively large head with a big mouth and prominent eyes.
Habitat: The Scorpionfish lives on rocky bottoms in shallow or deep waters. It lives on shrimps, crabs and small fish.
Alimentary value: The fish has a tasty flesh but because of its size it is mostly used to prepare fish stock.
Fishing methods: Both amateur and professional fishermen should be able to recognize this fish since it has venomous dorsal fin spines.

M: *Sparlu*

E: **Annular Sea Bream**

: *Diplodus annularis*

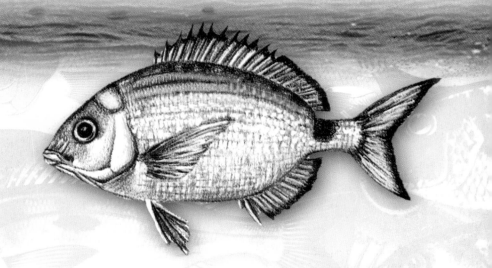

Size and weight: This fish can grow up to a length of about 20cm and a weight of about 200g.
Characteristics: The Annular Sea Bream has an ovoid and flattened body. It has a silvery colour with black bands running down its flanks and a black blotch on the tail stalk.
Habitat: It lives close to rocky and grassy bottoms.
Alimentary value: This is low but it can be used to prepare fish stock.
Fishing Methods: The Annular Sea Bream is caught by use of the fishing rod or a reel rod, especially on rocky bottoms. It is also caught by the bottom line (*mitlaq*) especially on reefs.

M: Spnotta
E: European Seabass
L: Dicentrarchus labrax

Size and weight: This fish can grow up to a length of about 1m and a weight of about 10kg.
Characteristics: The Seabass has a dark brownish-grey colour on the back and silvery flanks. Its abdomen is white.
Habitat: This fish enters bays for short periods of time and then returns to deeper waters. This fish is encountered more commonly since when it started to be exploited by the aquaculture industry. The fish which manage to escape the nets are still young and seek refuge close to the coast.
Alimentary value: This fish has a very fine flesh. It is a fast grower in warm waters.
Fishing Methods: This fish is easily caught in trammel nets (*pariti*). Amateur fishermen use the trolling method (*sajd bir-rixa*). The fish which manage to escape the aquaculture nets are usually still young and are mostly found close to the coast, but if it manages to live for long and eats on other fish, its flesh becomes even better.

M: Stokkafixx
E: *Blue Whiting*
L.: *Micromesistius poutassou*

Size and weight: This fish can grow up to a length of about 40cm and a weight of about 1.5kg.
Characteristics: This fish has an elongated body with large jaws and prominent eyes. Its colour is blue on the back that fades to a silvery shine on its flanks.
Habitat: It is mostly found swimming close to the surface of the sea.
Alimentary value: This is very low.
Fishing Methods: Fishermen are not usually interested in catching this fish although it can be caught in nets.

M: Strilja
E: Derbio
L: Trachinotus ovatus

Size and weight: This fish can grow up to a length of about 30cm and a weight of about 4kg.
Characteristics: Its body is similar to the Amberjack. However it can be distinguished from the latter fish by the presence of small pectoral and pelvic fins. It is also more silvery in colour and has about six black blotches on the flanks.
Habitat: This fish lives close to the surface of the sea in deep waters.
Alimentary value: Its flesh is very good.
Fishing Methods: It is caught in nets but also by trolling (*sajd bir-rixa*). Sometimes it swims up to snatch a piece of bread floating on the sea, and if the bread is hooked to a float (*forka*), the fishermen will surely be surprised with the catch.

M: *Sturjun*
E: *Sturgeon*
L: *Acipenser sturio*

Size and weight: This fish can grow up to a length of about 3m and a weight of about 500kg.

Characteristics: This is considered to be a primitive fish with bony rays in the fins. It has a pointed snout that is concave in its upper side. It has two pairs of barbels protruding under the mouth. It has an elongated body and its tail has a longer upper lobe, similar to that of sharks. It has a dusky green colour above with a silvery underside.

Habitat: It lives in both shallow and deep waters. The fish can use its snout to look for bottom-living invertebrates.

Alimentary value: The flesh of this fish is very good and the eggs present in a pregnant female are used as caviar.

Fishing Methods: The Sturgeon is caught in trawl nets (*xbieki tat-tkarkir*), gill nets (*għeżula*) and trammel nets (*pariti*).

M: *Sultan iċ-Ċawl*
E: *Cardinal Fish*
L: *Apogon imberbis*

Size and weight: This fish can grow up to a length of about 15cm and a weight of about 30g.
Characteristics: The Cardinal Fish is similar in shape to the Damselfish. It is however red in colour and has two dark bands crossing the eye.
Habitat: This fish lives close to the coast but is much less common then the Damselfish.
Alimentary value: This is very low.
Fishing Methods: This fish can be caught by the use of the fishing rod or in pots (*nassi*).

M: *Tannuta*
E: **Black Sea Bream**
L: *Spondyliosoma cantharus*

Size and weight: This fish can grow up to a length of about 30cm and a weight of about 1.2kg.
Characteristics: This fish has a thick-set body. It has a small head with prominent eyes. It has a silver colour with darker stripes. It has brown or green shades.
Habitat: The Black Sea Bream lives in shallow coastal waters or down to 100m close to the sea bed.
Alimentary value: The flesh of this fish is very good but it is not often marketed.
Fishing Methods: It is mostly caught by bottom long-lines (*konzijiet tal-qiegh*) and on the bottom line (*mitlaq*).

M: Tirda, Boxbox, Buxih
E: Axillary Wrasse
L: Symphodus mediterraneus

Size and weight: This fish can grow up to a length of about 15cm and a weight of about 60g.
Characteristics: Since there are various species of this fish, colours may vary. These may include red, brown and green. The Grey Wrasse has a predominance of grey while the striped Wrasse has reddish, brownish, yellowish, or orange colours with a white band along its side.
Habitat: The Axallary Wrasse lives in shallow waters close to the sea bed.
Alimentary value: The fish is usually used to prepare fish stock.
Fishing Methods: The fish can be caught with the use of the bottom line (*mitlaq*). Larger species can be caught by the harpoon.

M: *Tonn*
E: ***Blue-fin Tunny***
L: ***Thunnus thynnus***

Size and weight: This fish can grow up to a length of about 3m and a weight of about 600kg.
Characteristics: The Tuna has a large head with prominent eyes. Its back is black, fading to dark blue on the flanks and a silvery white bally.
Habitat: Since this fish prefers warm waters, it lives close to the surface in summer and in deep waters in winter. It is caught in Malta between May and August.
Alimentary value: The Tuna has a very good flesh which is very popular among Maltese.
Fishing Methods: The surface long-line (*konz tal-wiċċ*) has been used to catch Tuna since the past 40 years. Since the Grand Master Pinto the *tunnara* was used. This consisted of a labyrinth of nets in which the Tuna used to enter but did not find its way out. Another method, which is now illegal, made use of large nets which used to be left to drift with the sea current. This fish is the dream of every amateur fisherman. If caught while trolling (*sajd bir-rixa*) it offers a tough challenge. A strong rod with a reel is used. Fish such as Atlantic Mackerel may be thrown into the sea to attract the Tuna behind the boat.

M: Traċna tat-Tbajja
E: Spotted Weever
L: Trachinus araneus

Size and weight: This fish can grow up to a length of about 30cm and a weight of about 200g.
Characteristics: This fish resembles the Lesser Weever but grows more and has venomous fins on its back.
Habitat: The Spotted Weever lives on sandy bottoms and eats on shrimps and crabs.
Alimentary value: The flesh of the Spotted Weever is good, but because it has venomous fins the housewife does not buy it.
Fishing Methods: This fish is often caught in tremmel nets (*pariti*), but it is also caught by the bottom line (*mitlaq*).

M: *Trilja Tal-Hama*
E: *Red Mullet*
: *Mullus barbatus*

Size and weight: This fish can grow up to a length of about 30cm and a weight of about 200g.
Characteristics: This fish has a big head and prominent eyes. It has two long barbles protruding from below its mouth. It has a red colour.
Habitat: This fish lives mostly in deep waters, on sandy sea beds.
Alimentary value: This fish has a very good and tender flesh. The only disadvantage this fish has is that it is full of small bones.
Fishing Methods: Since this fish lives close to the sea bed, it is best caught in trawl nets (*xbieki tat-tkarkir*). The net is left to drag on the sea bed for about 30 minutes while the boat is moving forward. When hauled in, the contents of the net are laid on the fishing vessel. Many fishermen are against this type of fishing as it can destroy the sea bed.

M: Trilja Tal-Qawwi
E: Striped Red Mullet
L: *Mullus surmuletus*

Size and weight: This fish can grow up to a length of about 20cm and a weight of about 200g.

Characteristics: This fish has a dark horizontal band by which it is distinguished from other species.

Habitat: This fish lives mostly in deep waters, on sandy sea beds.

Alimentary value: This fish has a very good and tender flesh. The only disadvantage this fish has is that it is full of small bones.

Fishing Methods: Since this fish lives close to the sea bed, it is best caught in trawl nets (*xbieki tat-tkarkir*). The net is left to drag on the sea bed for about 30 minutes while the boat is moving forward. When hauled in, the contents of the net are laid on the fishing vessel. Many fishermen are against this type of fishing as it can destroy the sea bed.

M: *Tumbrell*
E: *Frigate Mackerel,*
Bullet Tuna
: *Auxis rochei*

Size and weight: This fish can grow up to a length of about 70cm and a weight of about 2kg.

Characteristics: The body of this fish resembles a bullet as it tapers on both sides. In fact it is also called the Bullet Tuna. It has a dark blue back and its sides are silvery. The upper part of the body has a black wavy pattern.

Habitat: This fish lives close to the surface or in mid-sea waters.

Alimentary value: Many people complain that this fish has a dry flesh but this depends much on how it is cooked.

Fishing Methods: This fish hunts in huge shoals and so it can be caught by the use of nets. This fish is mostly popular with amateur fishermen who own a boat. The trolling method (*sajd bir-rixa*) is adopted. A line of 0.6mm in diameter is used and this can be as long as 200m. About 20 to 40 hooks may be used, attached to the main line via a nylon line of about 30cm and 0.40mm in diameter. A real feather or one made from nylon may be used.

M: Vopa
E: Bogue
L: Boops boops

Size and weight: This fish can grow up to a length of about 30cm and a weight of about 500g.

Characteristics: This fish has an elongated body with prominent eyes and big jaws. It is dark grey on the back and silvery on its flanks. It has some yellowish lines on its flanks.

Habitat: The Bogue lives close to coastal waters, especially in summer.

Alimentary value: This fish has a tasty flesh and makes a very good fish soup.

Fishing Methods: The fish is caught in large quantities in nets such as the tremmel net (*parit*) and gill nets. The most common way how the amateur fishermen cathes this fish is by the use of the fishing rod. Hooks size 12 are used and bread, shrimps, snails, cheese or worms are used as bait. It is the most popular fish caught by amateur fishermen and it is mostly caught late in the afternoon or when the sun is setting. The Bogue trap (*nassa tal-vopi*) is mostly used by those who own a boat. This latter method is used by both amateur and professional fishermen. The best time when to use these traps is early in the morning or after five in the afternoon.

M: *Xilpa*
E: **Salema**
L: *Sarpa salpa*

Size and weight: This fish can grow up to a length of about 50cm and a weight of about 1kg.

Characteristics: This fish has a rounded body and a small head. It has a silvery bluish-grey colour with golden-yellow stripes reaching from head to tail.

Habitat: It swims close to rocky bottoms. It lives on grass and small fish.

Alimentary value: This fish prefers living in muddy and polluted sea water and so many fishermen do not cook it. When cooked in lemon juice, however, it is edible. Younger specimens are used to prepare fish stock.

Fishing Methods: It is caught in nets and may also find itself entrapped in a pot (*nassa*). It is often caught by amateur fishermen by the use of the fishing rod. Bread with Herring or a particular grass called *sellieha* are used or bait.

M: Xirghien
E: Two-banded Sea Bream
L: Diplodus vulgaris

Size and weight: This fish can grow up to a length of about 30cm and a weight of about 600g.
Characteristics: This Sea Bream has a deep, oval and compressed body. The colour is silvery grey with a black band at the nape of the neck and another directly in front of the tail peduncle.
Habitat: This fish lives close to rocky sea beds.
Alimentary value: The Two-banded Sea Bream has a good taste.
Fishing Methods: It is often caught by the amateur fisherman by the use of the fishing rod or on the bottom line (*mitlaq*).

116

: *Xkatlu Komuni*
: *Angelshark*
: *Squatina squatina*

Size and weight: This fish can grow up to a length of about 2m and a weight of about 50kg.
Characteristics: This fish is compressed dorso-ventrally and widened at the sides. It has a marbled sandy-brown back.
Habitat: The Angelshark lives on sandy bottoms.
Alimentary value: The flesh of this fish is good but it is not popular.
Fishing Methods: It is caught by the harpoon during underwater fishing, and by the use of trawl nets (*xbieki tat-tkarkir*).

M: Żagħrun
E: Gulper Shark
L: Centrophorus granulosus

Size and weight: This fish can grow up to a length of about 1.5m and a weight of about 20kg.
Characteristics: The body of this shark is broad and somewhat flattened. It has the same typical characteristics of any shark. Its back is brownish in colour and the belly is light brown to white.
Habitat: The Gulper Shark lives close to the bottom in deep waters.
Alimentary value: The flesh of this shark is good.
Fishing methods: This fish is often caught in trawl nets (*xbieki tat-tkarkir*) and gill nets (*għeżula*). It may also be caught with the surface long-lines (*konzijiet tal-wiċċ*) used to catch the Swordfish and Tuna. Some amateur fishermen venture to catch this fish by using a particular technique. The fisherman holds a rod that is connected to a large buoy from which a metal cable projects vertically towards the sea bed. To this metal cable are tied large hooks that are baited with whole fish.

M: Żondu
E: Stargazer
L: Uranoscopus scaber

Size and weight: This fish can grow up to a length of about 30cm and a weight of about 200g.
Characteristics: This fish has a relatively huge head with small eyes on top. It has a cavernous mouth. It is brown in colour and has dark spots on its flanks.
Habitat: The Stargazer lives close to the bottom of the sea bed half buried in sand or mud. It feeds on cuttlefish, molluscs, shrimps and small fish.
Alimentary value: This is very low.
Fishing Methods: The Stargazer can be caught on sandy bottoms by the bottom long-line (konz tal-qiegh). It is also caught in nets. The fish can generate a small electric shock, especially when touched close to the eyes.

Fish Classification

Order and Family	Species	English	Maltese
Branchiostomidae			
Branchiostomidae	Amphioxus lanceolatus	Lancelet	Amfiossu
Myxionidae			
Petromyzonidae	Petromyzon marinus	Sea Lamprey	Qalfat
Squatiniformes			
Squatinidae	Squatina squatina	Angel Shark	Xkatlu Komuni
Squaliformes			
Echinorhinidae	Echinorhinus brucus	Bramble Shark	Murruna tax-Xewka
Squalidae	Dalatias licha	Kitefin Shark	Murruna Sewda
	Centrophor. granulosus	Gulper Shark	Żaghrun
	Centrophorus uyato	Little Gulper Shark	Mazzola tax-Xewka
	Etmopterus spinax	Velvet Belly Shark	Mazzola tal-Fanal
	Squalus acanthias	Spur Dogfish	Mazzola Griża
Oxynotidae	Oxynotus centrina	Angular Roughshark	Pixxiporku
Hexanchiformes			
Hexanchidae	Heptranchias perlo	Sixgill Shark	Murruna Seba Garġi
	Hexancgus riseus	Sixgill Shark	Murruna Sitt Garġi
Carchariniformes			
Scyliorhinidae	Scyliorhinus canicula	Smallspot Catshark	Gattarell tat-Tikek
	Scyliorhinus stellaris	Nursehound	Gattarell tar-Rukkal
	Galeus melanostomus	Blackmouth Catshark	Gattarell Halq Iswed
Triakidae	Mustelus mustelus	Smoothhound	Mazzola bla Xewka
	Mustelus asterias	Starry Smoothhound	Mazzolla tat-Tbajja
	Galeorhinus galeus	Tope Shark	Kelb il-Bahar
Carcharhindidae	Carcharinus plumbeus	Sandbar Shark	Kelb Griż
	Prionace glauca	Blue Shark	Huta Kahla
Sphyrnidae	Sphyrna zygaena	Smooth Hammerhead	Kurazza Komuni
Lamniformes			
Odontaspididae	Eugomphodus taurus	Spot Sand Tigershark	Tawru
	Odontapsis ferox	Smalltooth Tiger Shark	Silfjun
Alopiidae	Alopias vulpinus	Thresher Shark	Pixxivolpi
Cetorhinidae	Cetorhinus maximus	Basking Shark	Gabdoll
Lamnidae	Carcharodon carcharias	Great White Shark	Kelb Abjad

	Isurus oxyrinchus	Shortfin Mako	Pixxitondu
	Lamna nasus	Porbeagle Shark	Pixxiplamtu
Hypotremata			
Pristidae	Pristis pristis	Sawfish	Pixxisega
Rhinobatidae	Rhinobatus rhinobatus	Common Guitarfish	Vjolin
	Rhinobatus cemiculus	Blackchin Guitarfish	Kuntrabaxx
Torpedinae	Torpedo marmorata	Marbled Electric Ray	Haddiela Komuni
	Torpedo nobiliana	Electric Ray	Haddiela Sewda
	Torpedo torpedo	Eyed Electric Ray	Haddiela tal-Ghajn
Rajidae	Raja batis	Flatter Skate	Rebekkin Skur
	Raja fullonoca	Shagreen Ray	Raja Petruża
	Raja oxyrinchus	Longnose Skate	Rebekkin Geddum Twil
	Raja melitensis	Maltese Brown Ray	Raja ta' Malta
	Raja clavata	Thornback Ray	Raja tal-Fosos
	Raja asterias	Starry Ray	Raja tal-Kwiekeb
	Raja miraletus	Brown Ray	Raja Lixxa
	Raja radula	Rough Ray	Raja tar-Ramel
Dasyatidae	Dasyatis pastinaca	Common Stingray	Boll Komuni
	Dasyatis centroura	Rough-tail Stingray	Boll Denbu Ahrax
	Dasyatis violacea	Violet Stingray	Boll Vjola
Myliobatidae	Myliobatis aquila	Eagle Ray	Hamiema Komuni
	Pteromylaeus bovinus	Bull Ray	Hamiema Ras Twila
Holocephalidae			
Chimaeridae	Chimaera monostrosa	Rabbitfish	Fenek tal-Bahar
Acipenseriformes Isospondsyli	Acipenser sturio	Sturgeon	Sturjun
Clupeidae	Alosa fallax	Twaite Shad	Laċċa tat-Tbajja
	Sardinella aurita	Golden Sardine	Laċċa tal-Faxx
	Sardinella pilchardus	European pilchard	Sardina
	Sprattus sprattus	Sprat	Laċċa Kahla
	Sardinella maderensis	Med. Sardinella	Laċċa Ġewnah Iswed
Engraulidae	Engraulis encrasicolus	European Anchovy	Inċova
Argentinidae	Argentina sphyraena	Argentine	Arġentina
Solenichthyes			
Macroramphosidae	M. scolpax	Snipefish	Pixxitrumbetta
Sygnathidae	H. hippocampus	Shortnosed Seahorse	Żiemel il-Bahar

	H. ramulosus	Longnose Seahorse	Żiemel il-Bahar
	Nerophis maculatus	Red banded Pipefish	Gremxula Hamra
	Nerophis ophidion	Straight nose Pipefish	Gremxula Irqiqa
	Syngnathus phlegon	Blue Pipefish	Gremxula Kahla
	Syngnathus acus	Great Pipefish	Gremxula Hoxna
	Syngnathus abaster	Short Snout Pipefish	Gremxula Halq Qasir
	Syngnathus typhle	Deep Nose Pipefish	Gremxula Halq Gholi

Myctophida

Chlorophthalmidae	C. agassizi	Short nose Greeneye	Panjol
Cyprinodontidae	Aphanius fasciatus	Killifish	Bużaqq
Synodontidae	Synodus saurus	Lizardfish	Skalm

Anguilliformes

Anguillidae	Anguilla anguilla	Common eel	Sallura
Congridae	Conger conger	Medi. Conger	Gringu
	Arisoma balearicum	Balearic Conger Eel	Morina Falza
Muraenidae	Muraena helena	Med. Moray	Morina
	Gymnothorax unicolor	Brown Moray Eel	Morina Kannella
Nettastomatidae	Nettastoma melanurum	Blackfin Sorcerer	Papra
Ophichthidae	Ophisurus serpens	Longjaw Snake Eel	Serp Halqu twil
	Arterichthus caecus	European Finless Eel	Gringu bla Ġwienah
	Dalophis imberbis	Armless Snake Eel	Gringu Serp
	Echelus myrus	Bluntnose Snake Eel	Gringu tar-Ramel
	Ophichthus rufus	Rufus Snake Eel	Serp Halqu Qasir

Belonoformes

Belonidae	Belone belone	Garfish	Imsella
	Tylosurus acus	Needlefish	Imsella Imprerjali
Scomberosocidae	Scomberox saurus	Atlantic Saury	Kastardella
Exocoetidae	Cheillopogon heterurus	Flying fish	Rondinella Komuni
	Hirundichthys rondeleti	Flying fish	Rondinella Rara

Anacanthini

Merluccidae	Merluccius merluccius	Hake	Marlozz
Gadidae	Gadiculus argenteus	Silvery pout	Nemusa
	Micromesis. poutassou	Blue Whiting	Stokkafixx
	Trisopterus minutus	Poor Cod	Bakkaljaw
	Gaidropsarus medi.	Shore Rockling	Ballottra tal-Bahar

	Scientific name	Common name	Maltese name
	G. vulgaris	Three-beard Rockling	Ballottra tat-Tikek
	Molva dipterygia	Blue Ling	Linarda
	Phycis blennoides	Greater Forkbeard	Lipp Abjad
	Phycis phycis	Forkbeard	Lipp tal-Qawwi
Trachipteridae	T. Trachypterus	Ribbonfish	Fjamma
	Zu cristatus	Scalloped Ribbonfish	Fjamma Rasha Kbira
Berycomorphi			
Trachichthyidae	Hoplostethus medi.	Rosy Soldierfish	Ġurdien tal-Warda
Zeomorphi			
Caproidae	Capros aper	Boarfish	Minfah
Zeidae	Zeus faber	John Dory	Pixxi San Pietru
Percomorphi			
Sphyraenidae	Sphyraena sphyraena	European Barracuda	Lizz
	Sphyraena chrysotaenia	Bluntjaw Barracuda	Lizz ta' l-Vant
Atherinidae	Atherina hepsetus	Common Sand Smelt	Kurunella
	Atherina boyeri	Boyer's Sand Smelt	Kurunella Ghajn Kbar
	Atherina presbyter	Silverside	Kurunella
Mugilidae	Chelon labrosus	Thick-lipped Mullet	Mulett Kaplat
	Liza Aurata	Golden-grey Mullet	Mulett tal-Misluta
	Liza ramada	Thin-lipped Mullet	Mulett ta' l-Imċarrat
	Liza saliens	Leaping Grey Mullet	Mulett Buri
	Mugil cephalus	Flatheaded Grey Mullet	Mulett ta' l-Iswed
	Oedalechilus labeo	Boxlip Mullet	Mulett Bobin
Apogonidae	Apogon imberbis	Cardinal Fish	Sultan iċ-Ċawl
Serranidae	Anthias anthias	Swallowtail Seaperch	Pixxiroża tar-Rigi
	Callanthias ruber	Parrot Seaperch	Pixxiroża ta' l-Għajn
	Epinephelus aeneus	Bronze Grouper	Dott tal-Faxxi
	E. alexandrinus	Golden Grouper	Dott Tebgha Safra
	Epinephelus caninus	Dog Toothed Grouper	Dott Iswed
	Epinephelus guaza	Dusky Grouper	Ċerna
	Mycteroperca rubra	Comb Grouper	Ċawlun
	Polyprion americanus	Wreckfish	Hanżir
	Serranus cabrilla	Comber	Serran
	Serratus hepatus	Brown Comber	Hanżir Burqax
	Serranus scriba	Painted Comber	Burqax

Moronidae	Dicentrarchus labrax	European Seabass	Spnotta
	Dicentrarchus punctatus	Spotted Seabass	Spnotta tat-Tbajja
Pomatomidae	Pomatomus saltator	Bluefish	Serra tas-Snien
Gempylidae	Ruvettus pretiosus	Escolar	Ruvett
Carangidae	Trachurus medi.	Med. Horse Mackerel	Sawrell Ghajn Kbar
	Trachurus picturatus	Blue Jack Mackerel	Sawrella Kahla
	Trachurus trachurus	European Scad	Sawrella
	Caranx rhoncus	False Scad	Sawrella Tikka Sewda
	Pseudocaranx dentex	Gruelly Jack	Sawrella Imperjali
	Caranx crysos	Medi. Trevally	Sawrella Denb Iswed
	Alepes djedaba	Shrimp Scad	Sawrell Imperjali Ċatt
	Alectis alexandrinus	Alexandrian Pompano	Sawrella Afrikana
	Campogramma glycos	Vadigo	Serra hoxna
	Lichia amia	Leerfish	Serra
	Seriola dumerili	Greater Amberjack	Ċervjola
	Seriola samstriata	Lesser Amberjack	Ċervjola tal-Faxxi
	Trachinotus ovatus	Derbio	Strilja
	Naucrates ductor	Pilotfish	Fanfru
Mullidae	Pseudopeneus barber.	Goatfish	Trilja ta' Lvant
	Mullus barbatus	Red Mullet	Trilja bla Faxxi
	Mullus surmuletus	Striped Red Mullet	Trilja tal-Faxxi
Bramidae	Brama brama	Ray's Bream	Pixxiluna
Sparidae	Salpa salpa	Saupi	Xilpa
	Boops boops	Bogue	Vopa
	Dentex dentex	Common Dentex	Denċi
	D. macrophthalmus	Large Eye Dentex	Denċi ta' l-Ghajn
	Dentex gibbosus	Pink Dentex	Denċi Hotbi
	Diplodus annularis	Annular Sea Bream	Sparlu
	Diplodus sargus	White Sea Bream	Sargu
	Diplodus vulgaris	Twobanded Sea Bream	Xirghien
	Diplodus puntazzo	Sharpsnout Sea Bream	Moghża
	Diplodus cervinus	Zebra Sea Bream	Sargu Iswed
	Oblada melanura	Saddled Bream	Kahlija
	Spondyl. cantharus	Black Sea Bream	Tannuta
	Sparus aurata	Gilthead Sea Bream	Awrata

	Pagellus acarne	Axillary Sea Bream	Bażuga
	Pagellus centrodontus	Red Sea Bream	Paġella tal-Garġi
	Pagellus bogaraveo	Blue-spotted Bream	Bażuga
	Pagellus erythrinus	Pandora	Paġella Hamra
	Pagrus auriga	Red-banded Bream	Pagru Hamrani
	Pagrus erehrenbergi	Blue Spotted Bream	Pagru Rar
	Pagrus pagrus	Common Sea Bream	Pagru Komuni
	Lithognathus mormyrus	Striped Sea Bream	Mingus
Centracanthidae	Centracanthus cirrus	Plain Picarel	Arznella Rara
	Spicara flexuosa	Small-spotted Picarel	Arznell/Munqar
	Spicara maena	Blotched Picarel	Pajżana
	Smaris smaris	Picarel	Arznella/Munqara
Sciaenidae	Sciena umbra	Brown Meagre	Gurbell Tork
	Argyrosomus regius	Meagre	Gurbell Rar
	Umbrina cirrosa	Bearded Croaker	Gůrbell tad-Daqna
Coryphaenidae	Coryphaena equisetis	Pompano Dolphin	Lampuka Rara
	Coryphaena hippurus	Dolphin Fiah	Lampuka
Cepolidae	Cepola rubescens	Red Bandfish	Fjamma Hamra
Pomacentridae	Chromis chromis	Damselfish	Ċawla
Labridae	Acantholabrus palloni	Scale-rayed Wrasse	Tirda Rara
	Labrus bimaculatus	Cuckoo Wrasse	Parpanjol
	Labrus merula	Brown Wrasse	Gharab
	Labrus viridis	Green Wrasse	Merlin
	Lapponella fasciata	Red Wrasse	Debba
	Symphonodus medi.	Axillary Wrasse	Boxbox
	S. cinereus	Grey Wrasse	Tirda Griża
	S. doderlini	Striped Wrasse	Tirda tar-Rig Abjad
	S. melanocercus	Black-tailed Wrasse	Tirda Denbha Iswed
	S. melops	Cork Wing Wrasse	Tirda Rasha Hamra
	S. ocellatus	Ocellated Wrasse	Tirda tal-Warda
	S. roisalli	Pink-lipped Wrasse	Boxbox Kannella
	S. rostratus	Long-snouted Wrasse	Buxih Ahdar
	S. tinca	Painted Wrasse	Tirda Mirlija
	Coris julis	Rainbow Wrasse	Gharusa
	Thalassoma pavo	Peacock Wrasse	Lhudi

	Xyrichthys novacula	Cleaver Wrasse	Rużetta
Scaridae	Sparisoma cretense	Parrotfish	Marżpan
Trachinidae	Echiichthys vipera	Lesser Weever	Sawt
	Trachinus araneus	Spotted Weever	Traċna tat-Tbajja
	Trachinus draco	Greater Weever	Sawt Kbir
	Trachinus radiatus	Streaked Weever	Traċna tal-Fond
Uranoscpidae	Uranoscopus scaber	Stargazer	Żondu
Siganidae	Siganus rivulatus	Spinefoot	Qawsalla
Trichiuridae	Lepidopus caudatus	Silver Scabbardfish	Ċinturin
	Trichiurus lepturus	Large-eyed Hairtail	Xabla Denbha Rqiq
Thunnidae	Thunnus thynnus	Atlantic Bluefin Tuna	Tonna
	Euthynnus alletteratus	Little Tunny	Kubrita
	Thunnus alalonga	Albacore	Alonga
	Euthynnus pelamis	Skipjack Tuna	Palamit
Scombridae	Auxis rochei	Frigate Mackerel	Tumbrell
	Scomber japonicus	Chub Mackerel	Kavall tal-Ghajn
	Scomber scombrus	Atlantic Mackerel	Kavall
Scomberomoridae	Sarda sarda	Atlantic Bonito	Plamtu
	Orcynopsis unicor	Plain Bonito	Plamtu bla Rigi
Xiphidae	Xiphias gladius	Swordfish	Pixxispad
Istiophoridae	Tetrapturus belone	Medi. Spearfish	Pastardella
Luvaridae	Luvarus imperialis	Louvar	Tonna Bajda
Centrolophidae	Centrolophus niger	Blackfish	Lampuka Torka
	Schedophilus ovalis	Imperial Blackfish	Huta tal-Bram
Stromateidae	Stromateus fiatola	Butterfish	Strilja Baghlija
Carapidae	Carapus acus	Pearlfish	Huta tal-hjar
Ammodytidae	Gymnan. cicerellus	Medi. Sand Eel	Ċiċċirella
Gobiidae	Aphia minuta	Transparent Goby	Makku
	Delten. quadrimaculatus	Four-spotted Goby	Mazzun Erbgha Tikek
	Gopius geniporus	Slender Goby	Mazzun Irqiq
	Gobius bucchichi	Bucchich's Goby	Mazzun Kannella
	Gobius cobitis	Giant Goby	Mazzun Kbir
	Gobius cruentatus	Red-mouthed Goby	Mazzun tad-Demm
	Pomatoschistus microps	Common Goby	Mazzun Komuni
	Gobius niger	Black Goby	Mazzun Iswed

	Gobius paganellus	Rock Goby	Mazzun tal-Port
	Pomatoschistus minutus	Sand Goby	Mazzun tar-Ramel
	Zoster. ophiocephalus	Grass Gòby	Mazzun Ghajnejn Kbar
Callionymidae	Callionymus lyra	Dragonet	Wiżgha ta' l-Ikhal
	Callionymus risso	Black-spot Dragonet	Wiżgha Tikek Suwed
	Callionymus maculatus	Spotted Dragonet	Wiżgha Tikek
	Callionymus pusillus	Small Dragonet	Wiżgha Żghira
Blennidae	Aidablennius sphinx	Sphinx Blenny	Budakkra Lewn Żebbuġ
	Blennius ocellaris	Butterfly Blenny	Budakkra ta' l-Ghajn
	Lipophyrs trigloides	Small Shanny	Bużullieqa
	Lipophyrs pholis	Shanny	Bużullieqa
	Lipophrys pavo	Crested Blenny	Budakkra ta' l-Ghalla
	Blennius basilicus	Zebra Blenny	Żebra
	Parablenn. gattorugin	Tompot Blenny	Budakkra tal-Qawwi
	Parablenn. sanguinoletus	Red-speckled Blenny	Budakkra Hamra
	Parablenn. incognitus	(No name)	(Mhemx isem)
	Parablenn. tentacularis	Horned Blenny	Budakkra Kannella
	Parablenn. zvonimiri	Zvonimir's Blenny	Budakkra tal-Qrun
	Blennius nigriceps	Black-headed Blenny	Bużullieqa Hamra
Clinidae	Clinitrachus argentatus	Silver Clinid	Budakkra tal-Fidda
Tripteriigidae	Tripterygion minor	Small-scaled Blenny	Bud. Żghira Ras Sewda
	Tripter. tripteronotus	Black-headed Blenny	Bud. rasha Sewda
Ophidiidae	Ophidion barbatum	Bearded Ophidion	Ballottra tal-Hama
	Ophidion rochei	Dark Ophidion	Ballottra tal-Bahar
	Parophidion vassalli	Cuskeel	Ballottra Hamranija
Peristediidae	Peristed. cataphractum	Armed Gurnard	Pixxikornut
Triglidae	Aspitrigla cuculus	Red Gurnard	Żumbrell Ghadma
	Eutrigla gurnurdus	Grey Gurnard	Gallina Griża
	Aspitrigla obscura	Longfin Gurnard	Żumbrell Spanjulett
	Lepidotrigla cavillone	Large-scaled Gurnard	Żumbrell Ahrax
	Trigloporus lastivosa	Streaked Gurnard	Gallinetta tar-Rigi
	Trigla lucerna	Tub Gurnard	Gallinetta
	Trigla lyra	Piper Gurnard	Gallina Ghadma
Scorpaenidae	Helicolen. dactylopterus	Rockfish	Ċippullazza ta' l-Ghajn
	Scorpaena notata	Small Scorpionfish	Skorfna tat-Tebgha

	Scorpaena porcus	Black Scorpionfish	Skorfna Sewda
	Scorpaena maderensis	Madeira Rockfish	Skorfna tal-Madejra
	Scorpaena scrofa	Red Scorpionfish	Ċippullazza
Dactylopteridae	Dactylopterus volitans	Flying Gurnard	Bies
Heterostomata			
Citharidae	Citharus linguatula	Spotted Flounder	Lingwata
Bothidae	Arnoglossus imperialis	Four-spotted Scaldfish	Lingwata
	Arnoglossus kessleri	Kessler's Scaldfish	Lingwata Tikek Suwed
	Arnoglossus laterna	Scaldfish	Lingwata Lixxa
	Bothus podas	Wide-eyed Flounder	Barbun
	Arnoglossus thori	Scaldfish	Lingwata tax-Xulliefa
	Scophthalmus rhombus	Brill	Barbun Lixx
	Psetta maxima	Turbot	Barbun Imperjali
	Buglossidium luteum	Yellow Sole	Lingwata Safra
	Microchirus variegatus	Thickback Sole	Lingwata tar-Rigi
	Microchirus hispidus	Whiskered Sole	Lingwata Harxa
	Solea solea	Common Sole	Lingwata Komuni
	Microchirus ocellatus	Four-eyed Sole	Lingwata ta' l-Ghajnejn
	Solea impar	Adriatic Sole	Lingwata Tikek Kohol
	Solea kleinii	Klein's Sole	Lingwata Tikek Bojod
Echeneiformes			
Echeneididae	Echeneis naucrates	Remora	Remora tal-Faxx
	Remora remora	Common Remora	Remora Komuni
Plectognathi			
Balistidae	Balistes carolinensis	Grey Triggerfish	Hmar
Tetraodontidae	Lagoceph. Lagocephalus	Pufferfish	Hmar Jintefah
Molidae	Mola mola	Ocean Sunfiah	Qamar
	Ranzania laevis	Oblong Sunfish	Qamar Tawwali
Xenopterygii			
Gobiesocidae	Lepado. Lepadogaster	Suckerfish	Buwahhal tat-Tentakli
	Diplecogaster bimaculata	Twospotted Clingfish	Buwahhal Rasu Qasira
	Lepadogaster candollei	Connemara Suckerfish	Buwahhal Rasu Twila
Pediculati			
Lophidae	Lophius budegassa	Lesser Anglerfish	Petriċa Żghira
	Lophius piscatorius	Greater Anglerfish	Petriċa Kbira